Introduction to Theology Workbook

Copyright ©2011 Credo House Ministries
109 NW 142nd St., Suite B, Edmond, OK 73003

ISBN-13: 978-1453896402
ISBN-10: 1453896406

BISAC: Religion/Christian Theology/General

This material is provided for students and instructors in The Theology Program. Use of this material is encouraged for personal study and for use in preparation of lessons, sermons, or other oral communication. This material may be quoted so long as the material is unaltered and credit is given to The Theology Program. It may not under any circumstances be reprinted for any reason or any purpose without the prior expressed written consent of the Credo House Ministries.

Certified instructors in The Theology Program are allowed to add to the material so long as approval is granted by The Theology Program developers. Pastors and teachers are encouraged to use the material in their teaching, but it must remain unaltered.

Unless otherwise noted, Scriptures are taken from the NEW AMERICAN STANDARD BIBLE, ©Copyright The Lockman Foundation 1960, 1962, 1963, 1968, 1971, 1972,1973, 1975, 1977, 1995. Used by permission. Scriptures are also taken from the NET Bible, © 1997–2003 by Biblical Studies Press, L.L.C. and the authors, and from HOLY BIBLE, NEW INTERNATIONAL VERSION®. Copyright © 1973, 1978, 1984 by International Bible Society. Used by permission of Zondervan Publishing House.

INTRODUCTION TO THEOLOGY
What is theology and why should I care?

"Jesus said to him, 'Love the Lord your God with all your heart, with all your soul, and with all your mind.'"
—Matthew 22:37

Question Outline

- Who are you and why are you here?
- What is The Theology Program?
- What is theology?
- Who is a theologian?
- How do we do theology every day?
- What are the different categories of theology?
- What is the Theological Process?
- What is epistemology?
- What is postmodernism?
- What questions are postmoderns asking?
- What is the postmodern view of truth?
- What is the modern view of truth?
- What is the Christian view of truth?
- What truths are relative and what truths are objective?
- What truths are essential for orthodoxy?
- How certain are you about your beliefs?
- What is the essential difference in Roman Catholicism, Eastern Orthodoxy, and Protestantism?
- Why are there so many Protestant denominations?
- What are the different sources for truth?
- What are the benefits and deficiencies of each source?
- How do the different sources interact to form our theology?
- Does God still speak today?
- What is the Continuationist view of prophecy?
- What is the Hard Cessationist view of prophecy?
- What is the Soft Cessationist view of prophecy?
- How do we do theology in our emerging context?

Course Outline

Syllabus 7

Session 1: Introduction to The Theology Program 23

Session 2: Defining Theology...33

Session 3: Categories of Theology 45

Session 4: Postmodern Epistemology 63

Session 5: Christian Epistemology 75

Session 6: Essentials of Theology 85

Session 7: Traditions of Christian Theology 97

Session 8: Sources of Theology...107

Session 9: Does God Still Speak Today? 123

Session 10: Unity and Diversity 133

Appendix: "Representing Christ to a Postmodern World"...................139

Key Terms 157

INTRODUCTION TO THEOLOGY
Syllabus

Course Description

This is a theological studies methods course. Its primary purpose is to teach you skills for developing a Christian mind, by helping you construct a solid foundation for thinking through life's most important issues. We will begin by establishing the reality and nature of truth and then learn that rightly interpreted Scripture is the final arbiter of truth. You will learn the about various sources for theology and the way that different people use and misuse these sources. This course endeavors to enable people to think theologically and construct a biblical worldview that makes the Christian's witness relevant to all people in need. This course is a prerequisite to all other required courses of theology.

Course Objectives

1. The student will understand that theology is more than just an academic discipline reserved only for professional theologians, but that it is a fountain from which all people may daily drink.

2. The student will know the different sources from which we derive our understanding of truth and direction.

3. The student will develop a broader perspective of theology in general and learn how theology is done within the Christian community.

4. The students will glorify God through their humble submission to His command to love Him with "all their mind" (Matt. 22:37).

5. The students will critically evaluate their own theological method and worldview by learning how to test and critique the validity of their core beliefs.

6. The students will critique various sources from which they derive their beliefs with the purpose of establishing the Scripture as their primary source for their beliefs.

7. The students will place greater confidence in theology and the process of doing theology.

8. The student will learn to value the unity and diversity of the Body of Christ.

Course Textbooks

Required:

- Grudem, Wayne. Systematic Theology. Grand Rapids, MI: Zondervan, 1994.

- Olson, Roger. Mosaic of Christian Beliefs. Downers Grove, IL: IVP, 2002.

- Bible (preferably New American Standard or NET Bible)

Course Requirements and Grading

This course can be taken at two levels: Certificate or self-study.

1. **Certificate Students:** Certificate students take the course for a grade to receive a certificate that can be applied towards the TTP diploma. You must pay the tuition, attend or view all ten sessions, and complete enough of the homework according to the grading system below to receive a passing grade. This applies to both online and campus students.

2. **Self-study:** Self-study students take the course for enrichment only. Homework is not required, although doing homework will obviously enrich your learning from the course.

Continuing Education Units (CEUs) may be offered depending upon the venue. Ask your instructor for more information.

Honors credit can be earned in this course by completing all the coursework and completing an additional reading assigned by the teacher. See bibliography for options.

Assignment Description - see course schedule for due dates

Viewing/Attending classes: Students are required to attend or view all ten sessions of the course. (All sessions for every course are posted on the TTP website and are available for viewing or for purchase.) Online certificate students: It is preferred that you view only one session per week so you won't get too far ahead of the rest of the class. While attending or viewing the sessions is required for all certificate students, it does not apply toward your grade and you cannot receive credit without it.

Ten hours of theological community time (online certificate students only): All online certificate students are required to spend one hour a week in the online TTP forums or in the voice/chat rooms provided. Each course will have a separate classroom in the TTP forums. In this classroom, you can accrue theological community time by asking or answering questions of other students, blogging your thoughts, discussing issues relevant to the course, or posting your answers to the discussion questions at the end of each lesson. Voice and chat rooms will be open each week where you can participate in live theological conversation with other students in your class (see website for details). While theological community time is required for all online certificate students, it does not apply toward your grade and you cannot receive credit without it.

1. **Reading:** Various reading assignments will be given during the ten-week period. Each student will be expected to read the material according to the ten-weeksession schedule provided in the syllabus.

2. **Scripture memorization:** Each student will memorize the passages provided on the Scripture memorization sheet in the syllabus. Once completed, the student will recite the memorized Scripture to a partner who will affirm the completion by signing the Scripture memorization sheet.

The preferred translations for all memorization in English are listed below:
- New American Standard
- NET Bible (available at www.bible.org)
- English Standard Version
- New International Version

3. **Case Studies:** The two case studies in the Workbook must be completed according to schedule. Online certificate students are to post their case studies online on the TTP forums. Your instructor will grade them online, marking them in red.

4. **Vocabulary Quizzes:** Two closed-book theological vocabulary quizzes will be given during the course of the semester. Online students can find these quizzes on the website. See schedule for due dates. Once the student looks at the quiz, he or she must take the quiz. In other words, you cannot look at the quiz, study the right terms, and then take the test.

Grading System

Complete 1 of 4	Complete 2 of 4	Complete 3 of 4	Complete 4 of 4	Complete all 4 plus honors reading
D	*C*	*B*	*A*	*A* *with honors*

Schedule

Session No.	Session Date	Session Topic	Assignments	Due Dates
1		Introduction to The Theology Program	Reading Assignment: *Mosaic of Christian Belief*, pp. 11–27; *Systematic Theology* pp. 21–43	Session 2
2		Defining Theology		Session 3
3		Categories of Theology	Reading Assignment: *Representing Christ to a Postmodern World* (contained in Workbook)	Session 4
4		Postmodern Epistemology		Session 5
5		Christian Epistemology	Reading Assignment: *Systematic Theology*, pp. 105–126 Case Study #1 Vocabulary Quiz #1	Session 6
6		Essentials of Theology		Session 7
7		Traditions of Christian Theology	Reading Assignment: *Systematic Theology*, pp. 47–53; *Mosaic of Christian Belief*, pp. 49–69	Session 8
8		Sources of Theology	Read Assignment: *Mosaic of Christian Belief*, 71–88	Session 9
9		Does God Still Speak Today?	Reading Assignments: *Mosaic of Christian Belief*, 29–48	Session 10
10		Unity and Diversity	Case Study #2 Vocabulary Quiz #2	One week after session 10

Bibliography for Introduction to Theology

Required Reading

Grudem, Wayne. Systematic Theology. Grand Rapids, MI: Zondervan, 1994.

Olson, Roger. Mosaic of Christian Beliefs. Downers Grove, IL: IVP, 2002.

Essential Reading

Elwell, Walter A., ed. Evangelical Dictionary of Theology. Grand Rapids, MI: Baker Book House Company, 2001.

*Moreland, J. P. Love Your God with All Your Mind. Colorado Springs, CO: NavPress, 1997.

Ryrie, Charles C. Basic Theology: A Popular Systematic Guide to Understanding Biblical Truth. Wheaton, IL: Victor Books, 1986.

Suggested Reading

Beckwith, Francis. Relativism: Feet Firmly Planted in Mid-Air. Grand Rapids, MI: Baker, 1998.

Berkhof, Louis. Systematic Theology. Grand Rapids, MI: William B. Eerdmans Publishing Company, 1996.

Carson, D. A., ed. Telling the Truth: Evangelizing Postmoderns. Grand Rapids, MI: Zondervan Publishing House, 2000.

Erickson, Millard J. Christian Theology. Grand Rapids, MI: Baker Book House Company, 1998.

_____. Postmodernizing the Faith. Grand Rapids, MI: Baker Book House Company, 1998.

Enns, Paul. The Moody Handbook of Theology. Chicago, IL: Moody Press, 1989.

Geisler, Norman. Systematic Theology: Volume One, Introduction, Bible. Minneapolis, MN: Bethany House, 2002.

Grenz, Stanley and John Franke, Beyond Foundationalism. Louisville, KY: John Knox Press, 2001.

* Groothuis, Douglas. Truth Decay: Defending Christianity Against The Challenges of Postmodernism. Downers Grove, IL: InterVarsity Press, 2000.

**Guiness, OS. Time for Truth: Living Free In A World Of Lies, Hype & Spin. Grand Rapids, MI: Baker Book House Company, 2000.

John Hannah, Our Legacy. Colorado Springs, CO: Navpress, 2001.

House, H. Wayne. Charts of Christian Theology & Doctrine. Grand Rapids, MI: Zondervan Publishing House, 1992.

McGrath, Alister E. Christian Theology, An Introduction. Malden, MA: Blackwell Publishers, 1998.

Noll, Mark. Scandal of the Evangelical Mind. Grand Rapids, MI: Eerdmans, 1994.

*Sire, James. Habits of the Mind. Colorado Springs, CO: IVP, 2000.

**Stott, John. Your Mind Matters. Colorado Springs, CO: IVP, 1973.

Honors Reading

Read one book marked with a single asterisk (*) or read all books marked with double asterisks (**).

Student Name _____

Scripture Memorization Sheet

• Deut. 18:18-22 (summarize the message in your own words)

• Deut. 13:1-3

• Rom. 1:18-20

• Heb. 1:1-2

• Matt. 22:37-38

• Deut. 29:29

• Jn.17:17

• Num. 23:19

I _____ have listened to _____
and confirm that he or she has recited the above Scriptures to me without any aid.
Signature_____

Case Study 1: The Theological Process

Introduction to Theology

This is going to be a "real life" case study. You are to find a person who would be willing to sit down and talk to you for thirty minutes to an hour. This person may or may not be a Christian. With your Workbook in hand the topic of your conversation is going to be explaining the theological process in session 3.

- Ask these questions before you begin:

    1. What is Theology?
    2. How does a person come to an understanding of theology?
    3. What common mistakes do you think that a person commits with regards to the Bible and theology?

- After this, explain the different categories of theology.

- Then go through the theological process chart and the charts explaining the common mistakes that people make with regard to the use of the Bible in this process.

The object of this assignment is to help people understand the theological process in relation to Scripture.

After you are done, write a half page to a page summary of the encounter and hand it in. Online student are to post their summary in their class forum. Grades will be based upon the completion of the assignment, not the effectiveness of the presentation. Everyone who completes this will receive credit for the case study.

Case Study 2: Essentials and Non-Essentials

Introduction to Theology

This is going to be a "real life" case study. You are to find a person who would be willing to sit down and talk to you for thirty minutes to an hour. This is to be one who professes to be a Christian. With your Workbook in hand, you are to explain what you have learned concerning the distinction between the essentials and nonessentials in session 6.

- Walk through the Quadrant of Objectivity and then ask the questions. Help the person to think through where they place them.

- Explain the Concentric Circle of Importance.

- Finally, explain the Chart of Certainty and ask the questions on that follow.

The object of this assignment is to help your friend understand how to think through issues that concern faith, objectivity, and certainty.

After you are done, write a half page to a page summary of the encounter and hand it in. Online student are to post their summary in their class forum. Grades will be based upon the completion of the assignment, not the effectiveness of the presentation. Everyone who completes this will receive credit for the case study.

"Jesus said to him, 'Love the Lord your God with all your heart, with all your soul, and with all your mind.'"
—Matthew 22:37

Session 1

INTRODUCTION TO THE THEOLOGY PROGRAM

Defining the "Rules of Engagement"
Who are you and why are you here?

Who you are and why you are taking this course?

1. **Practical Pricilla:** You are a person who has never seen the practicality in deep theological study. You are here to see if we can change your mind.

2. **Scared Susan:** Big words scare you. You don't really think that you are smart enough to be here. You are here this time, but you may not be here the next.

3. **Know-it-all Nick:** You already know everything. You are just here to see if we do—and to pick up where we leave off.

4. **Fundamental Fred:** You are the God-ordained guardian of orthodoxy. You are here to sit, with arms crossed, and protect.

5. **Want-an-answer Will:** You have a lot of questions. You are here not to do theology in community, but to write theology down with a pen and paper.

6. **Traditionalist Teri:** You want to learn, but your traditions and preconceived notions bind you. You are here to have your traditions confirmed to be true.

7. **Confrontational Carl:** You are not a believer in Christ or the Bible and have no intention of becoming one. You are here to argue.

8. **Struggling Sam:** You are a believer in Christ, but you have a lot of doubts and struggles. You have never had a safe place to express those doubts. You are here to see if this is the place.

9. **Curious Carla:** You are not really sure why you are here, but you're excited to find out.

We are all real people created by a real God, and we all have real struggles, real questions, and real convictions.

We are glad that you are here!

What is The Theology Program?

The Theology Program is an intense theological studies program, designed for busy people who may never go to seminary but who want deep theological training. While there are many great subjects, biblical and spiritual, that Christians can and need to study, our focus is on seven specific courses of systematic theology. Our desire is to teach people how to think by opening their minds to diverse views, learning from history, wrestling with difficult issues, and graciously engaging an increasingly relativistic and postmodern world.

Mission: Renewing minds and changing lives by purposefully guiding people through a study of historic and biblical Christian theology.

Goal: "Our goal is not so much to teach good theology, as important as this is, but to teach people to think."

What makes The Theology Program different?

1. Intensity in studies

2. Irenic theology

3. Intentional program design

4. Comprehensive coverage

5. Doing theology in community

Intensity in Studies

The Church must have an avenue of intense, interactive Christian education through a program which gives people an opportunity to learn at a level that other venues cannot provide. TTP endeavors to be this avenue.

The education program of the Church needs to include all of these in balance.

IRENIC THEOLOGY

Key Terms

Irenic Theology: Theology that is done peaceably, accurately representing all views, even when you oppose them.

Polemic Theology: Theology that is done in a warlike manner inside the Church, prophetically speaking against those with whom there is disagreement.

Apologetic Theology: Theology that is done to defend the faith against those who oppose outside the church.

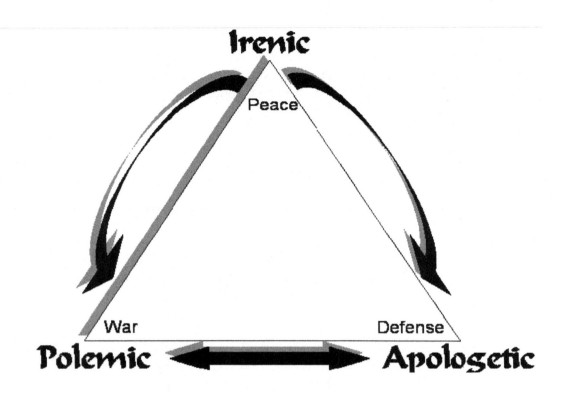

INTENTIONAL PROGRAM DESIGN

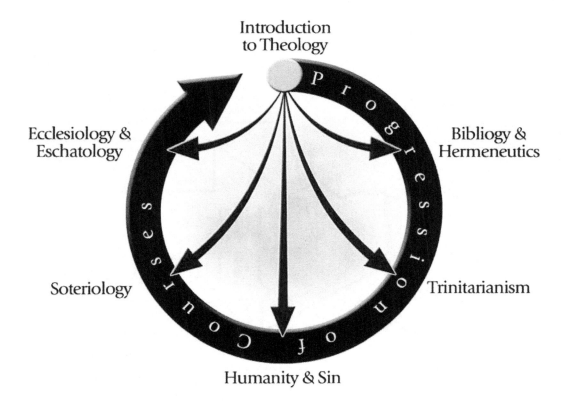

COMPREHENSIVE COVERAGE

In the courses, we will address all the relevant major issues, current and historic, of which we think people need to be aware.

DOING THEOLOGY IN A COMMUNITY

We believe that truth is not found in Spirit-illuminated individuals, but in a community of Spirit-illuminated individuals. Therefore, we believe that the Body of Christ, both alive and dead, must come together to understand theology, shaping it from many perspectives and differing experiences. This is doing theology in a community.

THE THEOLOGY PROGRAM LOGO

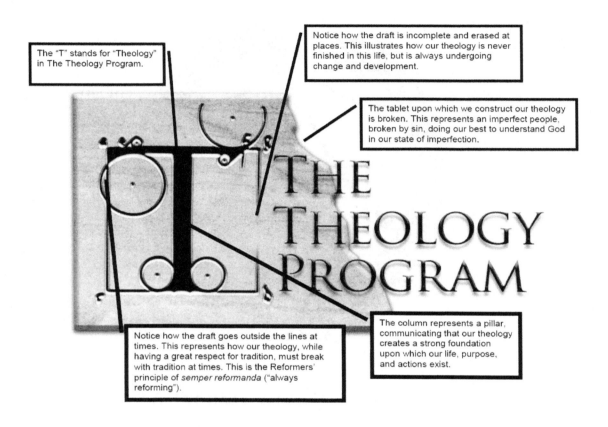

SESSION I: INTRODUCTION TO THEOLOGY

Group Discussion Questions

1. It was mentioned in class that the Christian faith is not a virtuous intellectual leap into the dark, believing that trusting God means that you check your brains in at the front door. How was Christian faith defined in the class lecture?

2. Read Isaiah 45:18–22; 46:5–10.

Do these passages encourage or discourage "blind faith"? Explain.

Pay particular attention to God's rebuke of the Israelites for worshiping other gods. Which took more "blind" faith, to worship a carved idol or to worship a God who predicts the future? Which kind of faith is God mocking them for having?

3. How does this change your thinking about what it means to have faith? Explain.

4. In the "Who are you and why are you taking this course" section, which of the nine types of people do you identify with most? Explain.

5. How do you think having so many different types of people with different perspectives, backgrounds, traditions, and passions will make this type of study better?

6. Irenic theology was described as theology that is done in a peaceable manner, accurately and humbly representing all views, even if you disagree with them. Polemic theology was described as theology that is done in a warlike manner inside the Church, prophetically speaking against those with whom there is disagreement. Do you think that Irenic theology is a better starting point for doing theology than Polemic theology? Explain.

7. Are there times when polemic confrontation is necessary? Explain.

Think of possible times when you have been personally rebuked for something sinful, destructive, or selfish. Did you need someone to peaceably come and represent your side, or did you need someone to give you stern rebuke?

8. How was your thinking most challenged by the lesson? Explain.

Session 2

DEFINING THEOLOGY

Traditions of Theology
Epistemology
Denominations
Experience
Eastern Orthodox
Cessationism
Pluralism
Relativism
Rationalism
Protestant
Modernism
Truth
Prophecy
Roman Catholic
Exclusivism
PROTESTANT THEOLOGY
Special Revelation
Continuationism
Postmodernism

What is theology?

What Is Theology?
Write a one or two sentence definition of theology:

> "The study or science of God."
> —Millard Erickson
> *Christian Theology* (Grand Rapids, MI: Baker, 2001), 22.

> "Rational discussion respecting the deity."
> —Augustine

> "The Science of God and of the relations between God and the universe."
> —A. H. Strong

> "Thinking about God and expressing those thoughts in some way."
> —Charles Ryrie
> *Basic Theology* (Wheaton, IL: 1986), 9.

> "The science of God or of religion; the science which treats of the existence, character, and attributes of God, his laws and government, the doctrines we are to believe, and the duties we are to practice; divinity; (as more commonly understood) the knowledge derivable from the Scriptures, *the systematic exhibition of revealed truth, the science of Christian faith and life.*"
> —Webster's Dictionary

Who is a theologian?

Anyone who has asked the ultimate questions of life:

- Why am I here?

- What is life?

- What happens after death?

- What is the difference between right and wrong?

- Why is there something instead of nothing?

SESSION 2: DEFINING THEOLOGY

> The question is not, "Who is a theologian?" but "What kind of theologian am I going to be?" Are you going to be a good theologian or a bad theologian? This is a more accurate question because, as one writer put it, "not all theologies are equal."
>
> —Source unknown

> "We live in what may be the most anti-intellectual period in the history of Western civilization... We must have passion—indeed hearts on fire for the things of God. But that passion must resist with intensity the anti-intellectual spirit of the world."
>
> —R. C. Sproul
>
> "Burning Hearts Are Not Nourished by Empty Heads," *Christianity Today* 26 (Sept. 3, 1982), 100.

There are basically six arenas in which we can do theology:[1]

1. Tabloid Theology

2. Folk Theology

3. Lay Theology

4. Ministerial Theology

5. Professional Theology

6. Academic Theology

---
[1] This is taken and adapted from Stanly Grenz and Roger Olsen's excellent book *Who Needs Theology?* (Downers Grove, IL: IVP, 1996), 22-35. The only addition is that of "Tabloid Theology."

SESSION 2: DEFINING THEOLOGY

Tabloid Theologian: One who constructs his or her theology based upon naïve hearsay information that has no basis in fact and very little, if any, evidence to be believed. Many times people are Tabloid theologians because of the theology's appearance of originality. As well, it can be "cutting edge" in many people's minds.

What are some examples of Tabloid theology?

Folk Theologian: One who uncritically and unreflectively constructs his or her theology according to traditions and religious folklore. The Folk theologian is often very dogmatic and militant about his or her beliefs.

What are some examples of Folk theology?

Why do you think that it is so hard for Folk theologians to learn?

Lay Theologian: A layperson, who constructs his or her theology and who, unlike the folk and tabloid theologian, is . . .
(1) more reflective upon learned theological concepts
(2) likely to formulate a system of beliefs which distinguishes between essential and non-essential doctrine
(3) more critical of unfounded traditions
(4) willing to use study tools

Ministerial Theologian: A layperson who constructs his or her theology and who, unlike the lay theologian is . . .
(1) educated in theological methodology
(2) able to use study tools and resources at a more effective level
(3) able to openly critique personal theology against competing models
(4) intent on devoting more time to reflection so that theological integration can take place.

Professional Theologian: One who constructs his or her theology and makes a living doing so. They usually. . .
(1) are didactically purposed toward lay and pastoral theologians
(2) conduct practical original research
(3) critically evaluate common theological trends and folk theology.

Professional theologians are often accused of "quenching the Spirit." Why do you think they receive this accusation?

SESSION 2: DEFINING THEOLOGY

Academic Theologian: A professional theologian who constructs his theology with an overly speculative and critical spirit. His dialogue can usually come only with other theologians. It is often called "Ivory Tower theology."

What are some examples of Academic theology?

Why do you think someone would want to be an Academic theologian?

> "Theology is for everyone. Indeed, everyone needs to be a theologian. In reality, everyone is a theologian—of one sort or another. And therein lies the problem. There is nothing wrong with being an amateur theologian or a professional theologian, but there is everything wrong with being an ignorant or sloppy theologian."
>
> —Charles Ryrie
> *Basic Theology* (Wheaton, IL: 1986), 9.

How do we "do" theology every day?

How do we "do" theology every day? In other words, how does our theology influence our daily routine?

1) When we think about God.

2) When we share the Gospel.

3) When we interpret the Bible.

4) When we get sick.

5) When we defend the faith.

6) When we plan for the future.

7) When we choose schooling for our children.

8) When we vote.

9) When we attempt to deal with sin in our lives.

10) When we decide on who we marry.

credo ut intelligam
"I believe in order to understand"

> This is a Latin phrase first put forth by Augustine, then popularized by Anselm of Canterbury (1033-1109). Augustine's full statement was "I don't understand so that I might believe, but I believe so that I might understand." This idea gives emphasis to the priority and necessity of belief in the Christian's intellectual pursuits. One cannot *truly* and *fully* understand spiritual matters unless he or she first believes them to be true.

SESSION 2: DEFINING THEOLOGY

fides quaerens intellectum
"Faith seeking understanding"

> This is a Latin phrase coined by Anselm of Canterbury (1033-1109) meaning "faith seeking understanding." This is one of the earliest definitions of theology. It starts with the assumption that we are believers and, as such, we are seeking to understand our beliefs better.

GROUP DISCUSSION QUESTIONS:

1. Reference was made to the quote from R.C. Sproul that we live in an antiintellectual culture. Another person once said that the sins of the culture become the sins of the Church. Further discuss the ways that the sin of antiintellectualism is evidenced in the Church.

2. Now discuss ways in which you tend to become anti-intellectual with regard to spiritual matters.

3. Why is it so easy to separate the intellectual life from the spiritual life? Discuss.

SESSION 2: DEFINING THEOLOGY

4. Many times I receive e-mails that include a short Scripture and prayer. The sender then attempts to persuade me to forward the e-mail to a certain number of people so that I can receive a blessing from God. How does this evidence Tabloid theology? Explain.

5. Discuss ways in which you have been influenced by Tabloid theology. Why is it so common for us to be Tabloid theologians?

6. Folk theology, unlike Tabloid theology, is rooted in traditions that have been passed on through various sources. But like Tabloid theology, Folk theology is baseless and naive. Further discuss and give examples of Folk theology.

7. In your notes there are examples of how theology affects a number of different areas in a section entitled "How do we do theology everyday." How are the issues listed below influenced by our theology?

When we get sick.

When we choose schooling for our children.

When we vote.

When we decide who we will marry.

8. How was your thinking most challenged by the lesson?

9. In the coming week, in what ways can you apply the lesson learned? Write them down.

Session 3

Categories of Theology

What are the different categories of theology?

Categories of Theology:

1. Systematic
2. Biblical
3. Historical
4. Philosophical
5. Creedal/Dogmatic
6. Apologetic

SYSTEMATIC THEOLOGY

1. **Prolegomena:**
Literally means "things which are spoken beforehand." Deals with the foundational issues of theology such as theological methodology, sources, and reasons for the study of theology.

2. **Bibliology:**
The study of the nature, transmission, canonization, and purpose of Scripture.

3. **Theology Proper:**
The study of God's existence, nature, and attributes. Sometimes called "Trinitarianism."

4. **Christology:**
The study of the person and work of Christ.

5. **Pneumatology:**
The study of the person and work of the Holy Spirit.

6. Anthropology:
The study of the purpose and nature of humanity, both in its pre-fall and postfall state.

7. Hamartiology:
The study of the nature, origin, and effects of sin on all creation.

8. Angelology:
The study of the nature and works of demons and angels.

9. Soteriology:
The study of salvation.

10. Ecclesiology:
The study of the nature of the Church.

11. Eschatology:
The study of the end times.

BIBLICAL	SYSTEMATIC
• Restricts the formulation of theology *only to the Scripture*.	• Formulates theology from *all sources of theology*, including Scripture.
• Sometimes will examine *the individual parts of Scripture* in order to formulate a particular theology that is *restricted to a certain time period and a particular people* (e.g., Pre-mosaic theology).	• Correlates the *entirety Scripture* to formulate a general theology *for all time and for all people*.
• Sometimes examines the theology of a *certain author* (e.g., John or Paul).	• Correlates information on a doctrine by examining the theology of *all the authors*.

SESSION 3: CATEGORIES OF THEOLOGY

HISTORICAL	SYSTEMATIC
• Restricts the formulation of theology *only to the history of the Church*. • Sometimes will examine *the individual periods of Church history* in order to formulate a particular theology that is *restricted to a certain time period* (e.g., Patristic, Medieval, and Reformation).	• Formulates theology from *all sources of theology*. • Correlates the *all of Church history* to formulate a general theology *for all time and for all people*.

PHILOSOPHICAL	SYSTEMATIC
• Restricts the formulation of theology *only to that which can be ascertained by reason*. • Sometimes will examine *the individual periods of philosophical history* in order to formulate a particular theology that is *restricted to a certain time period* (e.g., enlightenment, modern, postmodern).	• Formulates theology from *all sources of theology*. • Correlates the *all of philosophical history* to formulate a general theology *for all time and for all people*.

CREEDAL	SYSTEMATIC
• Restricts the formulation of theology *only to that of a particular religious institution or denomination*.	• Formulates theology from *all sources of theology* including the creedal statement of many institutions and denominations.

APOLOGETIC	SYSTEMATIC
• Formulates theology for the purpose of explaining and defending the faith to those outside the faith.	• Formulates theology for the purpose of creating a comprehensive and coherent understanding of various doctrines.

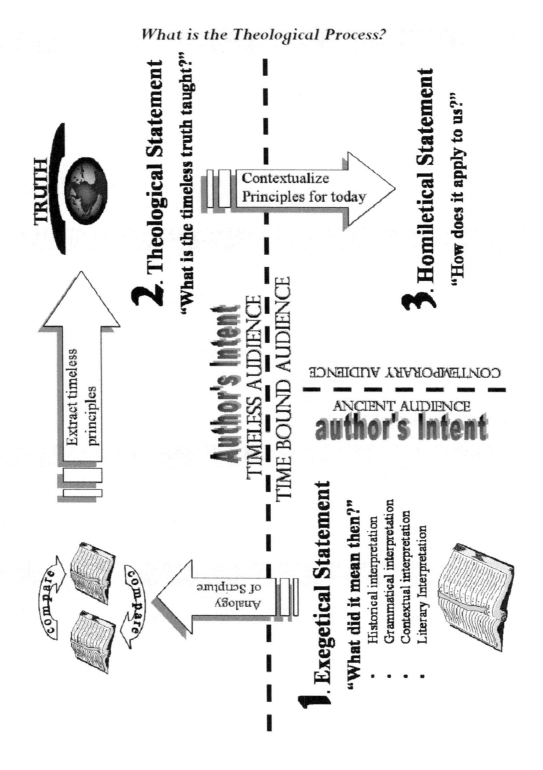

SESSION 3: CATEGORIES OF THEOLOGY

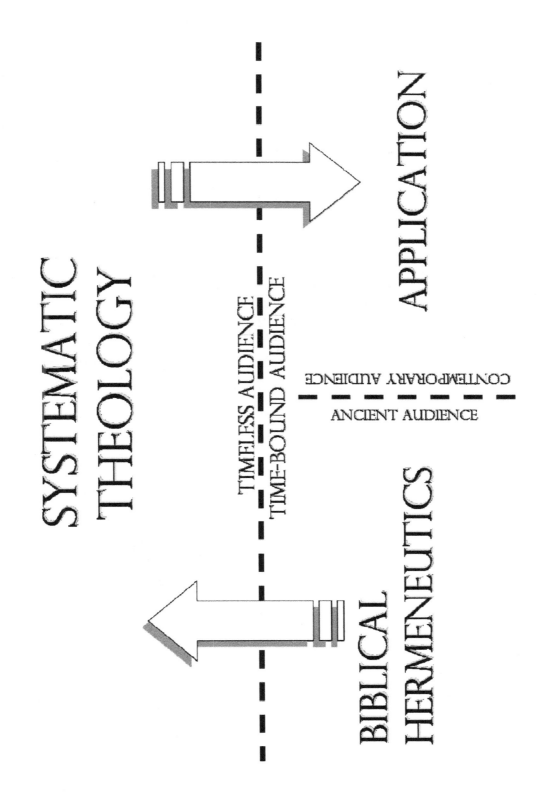

SESSION 3: CATEGORIES OF THEOLOGY

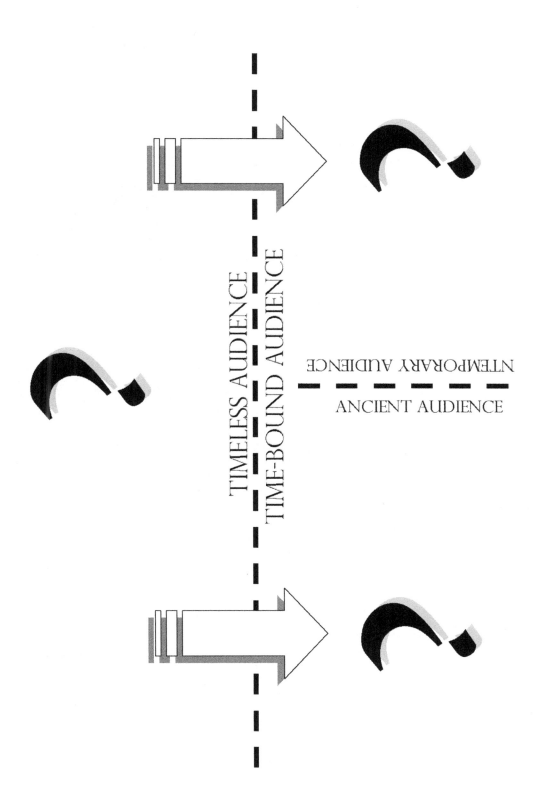

52 INTRODUCTION TO THEOLOGY

TIMELESS AUDIENCE
TIME-BOUND AUDIENCE
CONTEMPORARY AUDIENCE
ANCIENT AUDIENCE

SESSION 3: CATEGORIES OF THEOLOGY

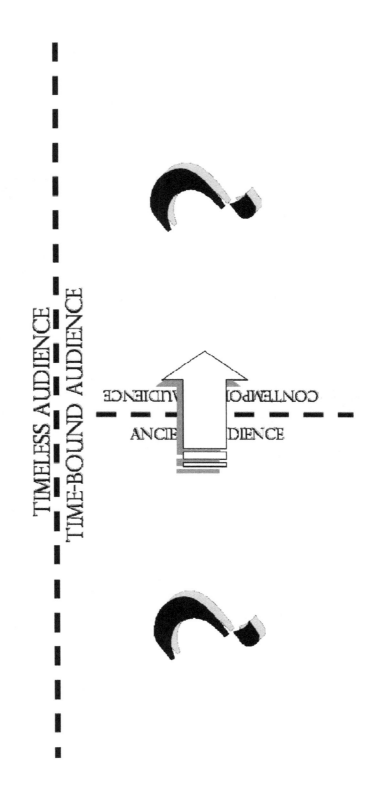

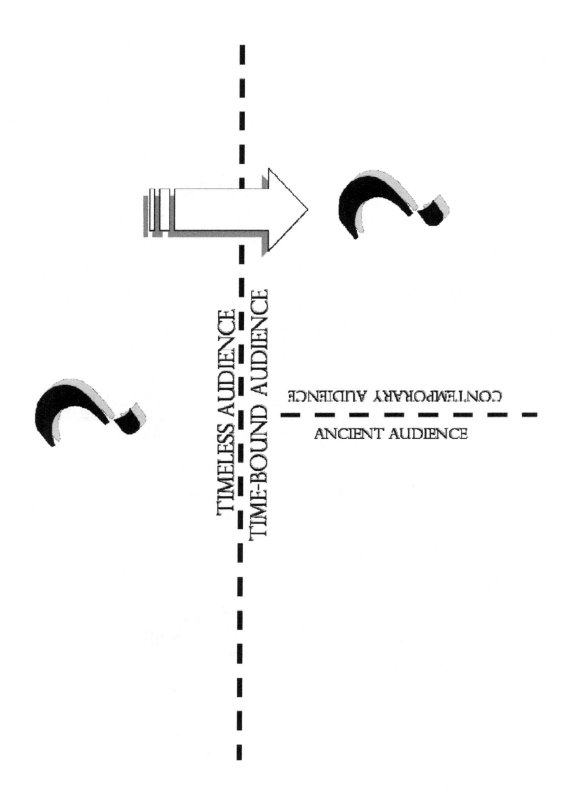

SESSION 3: CATEGORIES OF THEOLOGY

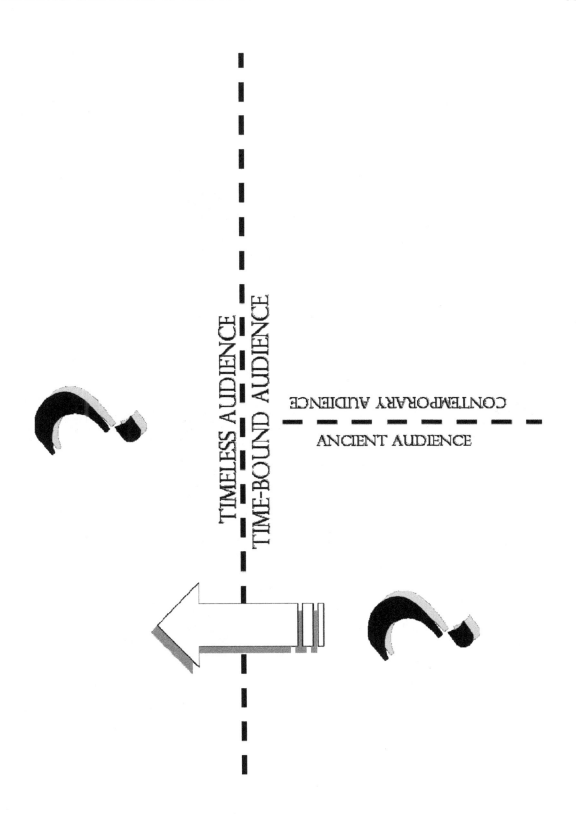

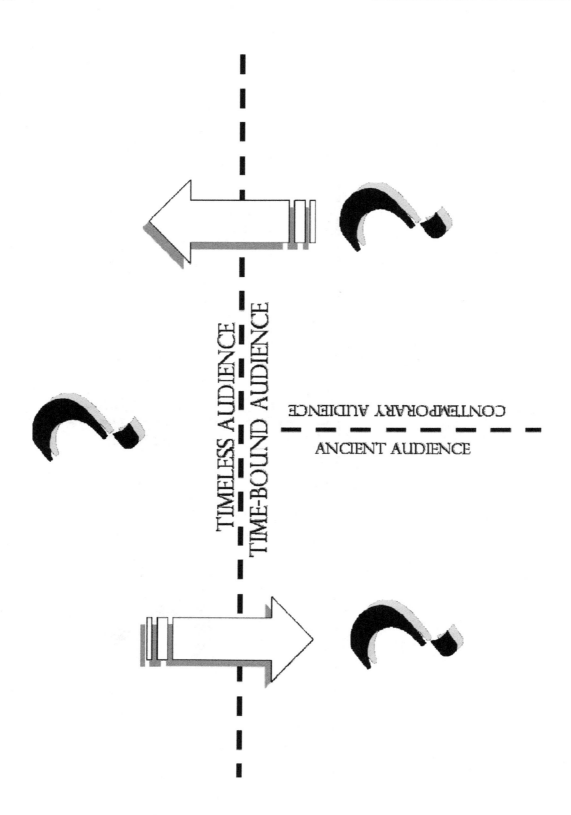

SESSION 3: CATEGORIES OF THEOLOGY

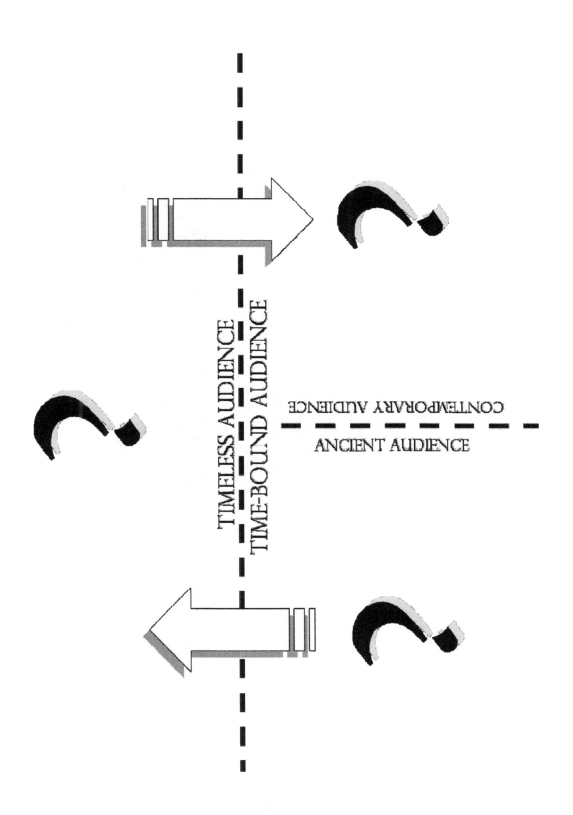

SESSION 3: CATEGORIES OF THEOLOGY

GROUP DISCUSSION QUESTIONS:

1. Many would say that when Christians do theology, they should do so objectively, using only the Bible as their source. Is this possible? Why or why not?

2. Some Christian apologists (often called Classical apologists) believe that using the Bible to convince an unbeliever of a Christian worldview is impossible because the unbeliever does not believe the Bible. Do you believe that this is true? Discuss.

3. Philosophical theology seeks to understand the world using nothing but what all people have in common—our reasoning capability. If someone you know did not believe the Bible but was searching for truth, how would Philosophical theology be beneficial?

4. Historical theology seeks the contribution of past saints to formulate theology. Some people do not seek the contribution of past saints, thinking that Christians do not need tradition, since it has misled us so many times.

How is this attitude arrogant and fallacious?

How is this attitude wise and cautious?

5. Systematic theology seeks to draw from all sources of theology. How does doing theology systematically help make the doctrine of God (for example) more complete?

6. Review Subjective theology. How have you experienced Subjective theology in your own personal life?

How have you experienced Subjective theology done in a small group?

SESSION 3: CATEGORIES OF THEOLOGY

7. It was said during the lesson that when reading the Bible "it does not matter what it means to you. It matters what it meant." How is this true? Discuss.

8. Discuss the difference between asking a) what does a Scripture mean to you? and b) how does a Scripture apply to you?

9. Review Irrelevant theology. Read Acts 1:26. The Apostles cast lots in order to replace Judas as an Apostle. How might an Irrelevant theologian apply this passage?

Give some other examples of how Irrelevant theology might be practiced.

10. Review Eisegetical theology. Give some examples of how you have practiced this type of theology.

Why do you think that we often interpret Scripture this way?

Session 4
POSTMODERN EPISTEMOLOGY

Understanding Our Changing Culture

What is Epistemology?

> "The theory or science of the method or grounds of knowledge."
> —Webster's Dictionary

> "The branch of philosophy that is concerned with the theory of knowledge. It is an inquiry into the nature and source of knowledge, the bounds of knowledge, and the justification of claims to knowledge."
> —Paul Feinberg

Walter A. Elwell ed., "Epistemology" in *The Evangelical Dictionary of Theology* (Grand Rapids, MI: Baker, 2001). 382.

Key Terms

Relativism: The belief that all truth is relative, being determined by some group.

Subjectivism: The belief that all truth is subjective, being defined by the perspective of the individual.

Skepticism: The belief that truth cannot be known with certainty.

Perspectivism: The belief that truth is found in the combined perspectives of many.

Pragmatism: The belief that truth is ultimately defined by that which works to accomplish the best outcome. "The end justifies the means."

Objectivism: The belief that truth is an objective reality that exist whether someone believes it or not.

Which best describes our culture today?

1. Relativism

2. Subjectivism

3. Skepticism

4. Perspectivism

5. Pragmatism

6. Objectivism

What is Postmodernism?

> "Christian's today cannot work with the same assumptions that we did just 20 years ago. At that time, people would join you in your search for absolute truth. It is different now. Today, before we begin to lead people to the truth of Jesus Christ, we may have to lead them to the truth of truth. Common ground must be created before the Gospel can be proclaimed"

SESSION 4: POSTMODERN EPISTEMOLOGY

> "Apologetically, the question which arises in the postmodern context is the following. How can Christianity's claims to truth be taken seriously, when there are so many rival alternatives, and when 'truth' itself has become a devalued notion? No-one can lay claim to possession of truth. It is all a question of perspective. The conclusion of this line of thought is as simple as it is devastating: 'the truth is that there is no truth'"
>
> —Alister McGrath
>
> *A Passion for Truth* (Downers Grove, IL: IVP, 1996), 188

Conversation Between Protagoras and Socrates (4th B.C.)

Protagoras: Truth is relative. It is only a matter of opinion.

Socrates: You mean that truth is mere subjective opinion?

Protagoras: Exactly. What is true for you is true for you, and what is true for me is true for me. Truth is subjective.

Socrates: Do you really mean that? That my opinion is true by virtue of its being my opinion?

Protagoras: Indeed I do.

Socrates: My opinion is: Truth is absolute, not opinion, and that you, Mr. Protagoras, are absolutely in error. Since this is my opinion, you must grant that it is true according to your philosophy.

Protagoras: You are quite correct, Socrates.

Self-defeating Statements

"I cannot speak a word in English."

"My wife has never been married."

"We cannot know anything about God."

"There is no such thing as truth."

"Truth cannot be known with certainty."

A short history of western civilization

Three periods:

1. Premodern (400-1600 A.D.)

2. Modern (1600-1900 A.D.)

3. Postmodern (1960-present)

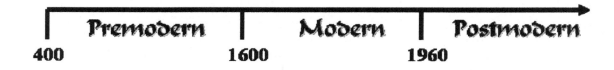

SESSION 4: POSTMODERN EPISTEMOLOGY

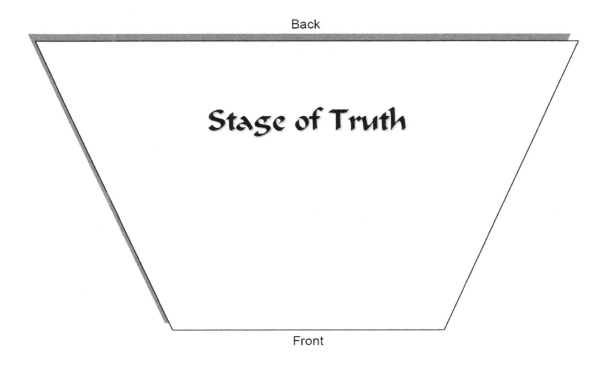

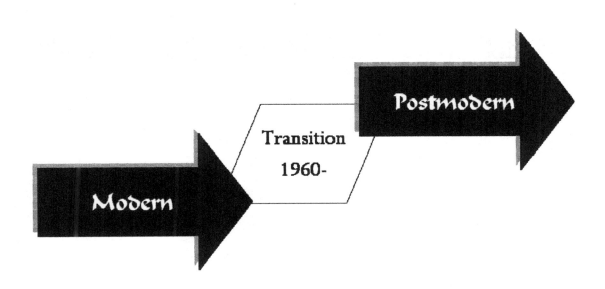

Modern Generation
— Preboomers
— Boomers

43%

Postmodern Generation
— Busters (Gen X)
— Bridgers (Gen Y)

57%

Modernism	Postmodernism
• Intellectual	• Anti-intellectual
• Reason	• Feeling
• Optimism	• Pessimism
• Hope for the future	• Despair for the present
• Objectivism	• Subjectivism/relativism
• Exclusivism	• Pluralism/inclusivism
• Science method	• Distrust in science
• Man is evolving	• Man is devolving

SESSION 4: POSTMODERN EPISTEMOLOGY

The Ideal Modern Man:[2]
Mr. Spock

- Spock is always logical and objective.

- Never acts upon feeling, because that would be "illogical."

"Physical laws simply cannot be ignored. Existence cannot be without them."

"Pain is a thing of the mind. The mind can be controlled."

The Ideal Modern Man Mocked:
Data

- Data is the "perfect" modern human.

- Despite his "perfection," Data . . .
  - Wants to be human.
  - Rebels against logic.
  - Attempts to develop emotions and feelings.

---

2 The illustration of Spock and Data is adapted from Stanley Grenz Primer on Postmodernism (Grand Rapids, MI: Eerdmans, 1996), 1-10.

- **Premodern:** "There's balls and there's strikes and I call them as they are."

- **Modern:** "There's balls and there's strikes and I call them as I see them."

- **Postmodern:** "They ain't nothing 'til I call 'em."

"In Postmodernism, there is no objective, universal truth; there is only the perspective of the group. . . . In postmodernism, all viewpoints, all lifestyles, all beliefs and behaviors are regarded as equally valid. . . . Tolerance has become so important that no exception is tolerated."
—Charles Colson

How Now Shall We Live? (Wheaton, IL: Tyndale, 1999), 23

SESSION 4: POSTMODERN EPISTEMOLOGY

GROUP DISCUSSION QUESTIONS:

1. Discuss the contact you have had with the postmodern mindset.

2. Some argue that those who say they believe that all truth is relative don't actually live this way. Explain why it is virtually impossible to live out a relativistic worldview.

3. Discuss the validity of this statement: "People are only relativistic when it comes to the issues of morals and metaphysics (God, spiritual things, etc.). They are not relativistic when it comes to the mundane."

4. Do you still see modernism's overly optimistic worldview in our society today? Give examples.

5. Empathize with people's despair caused by the failed claims of modernism.

6. Which way of thinking do you identify with most: Modernism or Postmodernism? How?

SESSION 4: POSTMODERN EPISTEMOLOGY

7. Why do you think that postmoderns are described as people who are in despair? How have you observed this?

8. In what ways would having a subjective or relative worldview cause you despair?

9. How was your thinking most challenged by the lesson? Explain.

Session 5
CHRISTIAN EPISTEMOLOGY

How does a Christian come to know truth?

What questions are postmoderns asking?

Modernist Objections to Christianity

1. What about all the contradictions?

2. God is just a crutch. Religion was invented by man.

3. Jesus was just a man.

4. The Bible we have today is not the same as when it was written 2000 years ago.

5. I don't believe in what I can't see.

6. Evolution has proven Christianity to be wrong.

7. The Bible is a myth full of fairy tales.

8. How did Noah get all of the animals on the Ark?

9. There is no such thing as miracles.

10. Do you really believe in the story of Adam and Eve?

Postmodernist Objections to Christianity

1. If God exists, why is there evil?

2. The Inquisition and the Crusades show that Christianity is oppressive.

3. Christianity is a way to God but not the only way.

4. Christianity is arrogant and exclusive.

5. How do you know that your Bible is better than other religious writings?

6. Why does God allow bad things to happen to good people?

7. What about those who have never heard?

8. The church is full of hypocrites.

9. Why would God send anyone to Hell?

10. The God of the OT is cruel, partial, and unjust.

Modernist	Postmodernist
Facts	Fairness
Rationality	Relationships
Evidence	Emotion

What is the modern view of truth?

SESSION 5: CHRISTIAN EPISTEMOLOGY

Modern View of Truth

Correspondence view of truth: (1) Truth is an objective reality that exists whether someone believes it or not, (2) and that objective reality is grounded in nature.

*True statements are those which correspond to that objective reality.
False statements are those which do not correspond to that objective reality.*

Law of non-contradiction applies

$$A \neq -A$$

at the same time and in the same relationship.

> **Key Motto**
> "Man can and will know all truth."

What is the postmodern view of truth?

Postmodern View of Truth

Relative view of truth: (1) Truth is a perspective reality that exists in the perspective of the individual or group, (2) and that perspective reality is grounded in time.

Law of non-contradiction does not apply

$$A = -A$$

at the same time and in the same relationship.

> **Key Motto**
> "The truth cannot be known

Religious Spin on Postmodern Epistemology

Universalism: The belief that all people, good or bad, will eventually make it to Heaven.

Pluralism: The belief that there are many ways to God that are equally valid.

Syncretism: The assimilation of differing beliefs and practices.

Inclusivism: The belief that salvation is only through Christ, but Christ may be revealed in other religions.

Vatican II (1962-1965) and inclusivism

"But the plan of salvation also includes those who acknowledge the creator. In the first place among these there are the Moslems, whom professing to hold the faith of Abraham, along with us adore the one and merciful god, who on the last day will judge mankind. Those also can attain salvation who through no fault of their own do not know the gospel of Christ or his church, yet sincerely seek god and, moved by grace, strive by their deeds to do his will as it is known to them through the dictates of conscience."

What is the Christian view truth?

SESSION 5: CHRISTIAN EPISTEMOLOGY

Christian View of Truth

Correspondence view of truth: (1) Truth is an objective reality that exists whether someone believes it or not, (2) and that objective reality is grounded in an eternal God.

The law of non-contradiction is a foundational necessity to all truth.

God cannot even violate this principle since it is a logical impossibility.

> ### Key Motto
> "The **secret things** belong to the Lord our God, but the **things revealed** belong to us and to our sons forever, that we may observe all the words of this law" (Deut. 29:29).

Christian truth must have a balance between the "things revealed" and mystery ("secret things").

Apophatic Theology: Theology that emphasizes mystery. Often called the "way of negation" (via negativa) or "negative theology," apophatic theology sees God, and much of theology, as beyond our understanding and, therefore, beyond defining through positive assertations. Finite people cannot say what the infinite God is but only what He is not. God is "uncreated," "immutable," "infinite," "immortal."

Cataphatic Theology: Theology that emphasizes revelation. Often called "positive theology," cataphatic theology seeks to understand God in positive terms, understanding that God communicates to us through language and concepts that are analogous to who and what He truly is ("analogy of language").

Cataphatic Theology	Apophatic Theology
"things revealed"	"secret things"
Modernism	Postmodernism
West	East
Rationalists	Mystics
Roman Catholic/Protestants	Eastern Orthodox

Responsible theology ⟶

> "Resolved, when I think of any theorem in divinity to be solved, immediately to do what I can towards solving it, if circumstances do not hinder."
> —Jonathan Edwards
> *Resolutions*, 11

SESSION 5: CHRISTIAN EPISTEMOLOGY

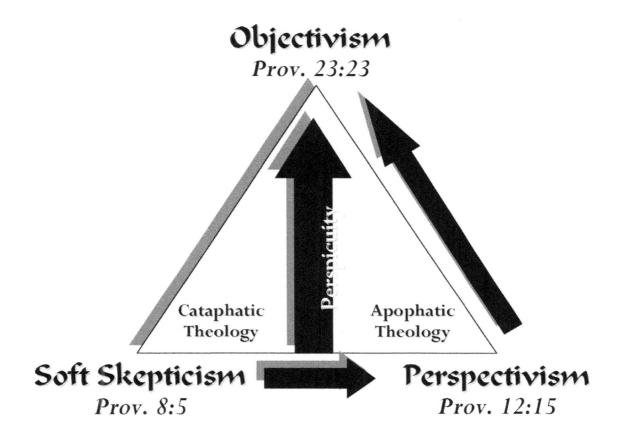

GROUP DISCUSSION QUESTIONS:

1. Reread the modernist objections to Christianity. Which objections have you heard the most? Which objections do you find the most difficult? Why?

2. Reread the postmodernist objections to Christianity. Which objections have you heard the most? Which objections do you find the most difficult? Why?

3. Do you know anyone who has died who you believe may be in Hell? How do you deal with this?

SESSION 5: CHRISTIAN EPISTEMOLOGY

4. The following question was asked during the last group discussion: "Which mindset do you identify with most: Modernism or Postmodernism?" Which do you identify with most now? If your position has changed, explain why.

5. How does the distinction between Cataphatic theology and Apophatic theology help you to understand how to approach theology? Explain.

6. Read Prov. 3:7; 12:1, 15; 18:1; 19:20. Why do you think that the Bible is so emphatic about having many advisors or counselors?

7. How does the individualism of America conflict with the instruction of the Proverbs concerning having advisors and counselors? Give examples.

8. To be perspicuous means "plain to the understanding especially because of clarity and precision of presentation" (Webster's). Name some teachings of Scripture that are plain to the understanding.

9. How was your thinking most challenged by the lesson? Explain.

Session 6

DEFINING ESSENTIALS AND NON-ESSENTIALS

What is the sine quo non of Christianity?

What truths are relative and what truths are objective?

Discussion of paper "Representing Christ to a Postmodern World"

Quadrant of Objectivity

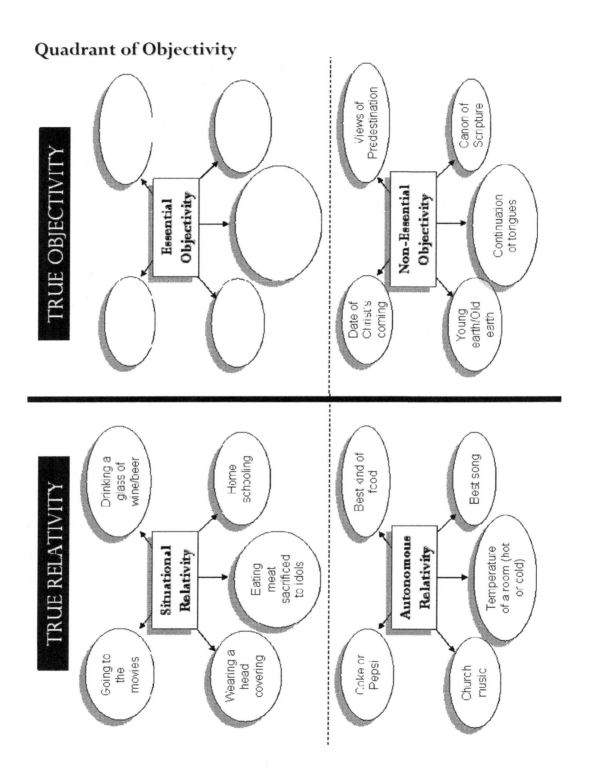

SESSION 6: DEFINING ESSENTIALS AND NON-ESSENTIALS

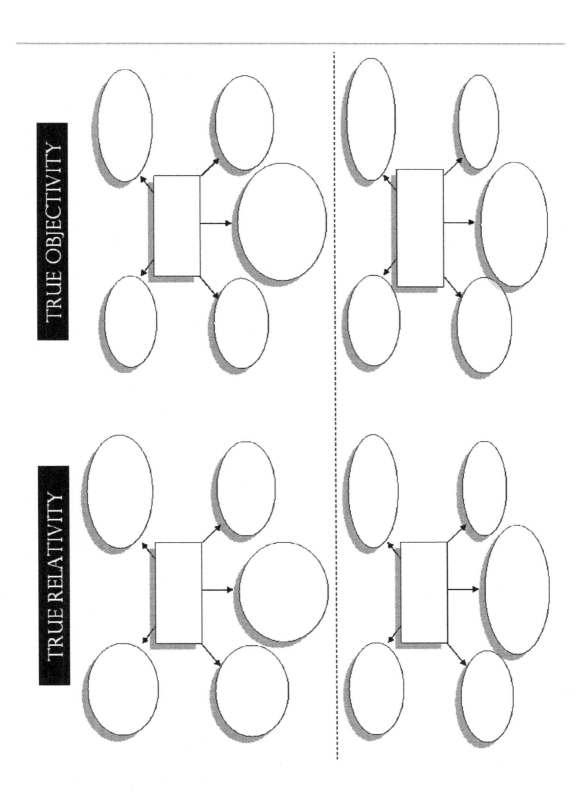

Where would you place these on the quadrant?

• Belief in the doctrine of the Trinity? Why?

• Smoking? Why?

• Eating healthy and exercising? Why?

• Getting intoxicated? Why?

• Having your mind altered by anti-depressants? Why?

What truths are essential for orthodoxy?

Concentric Circle of Importance

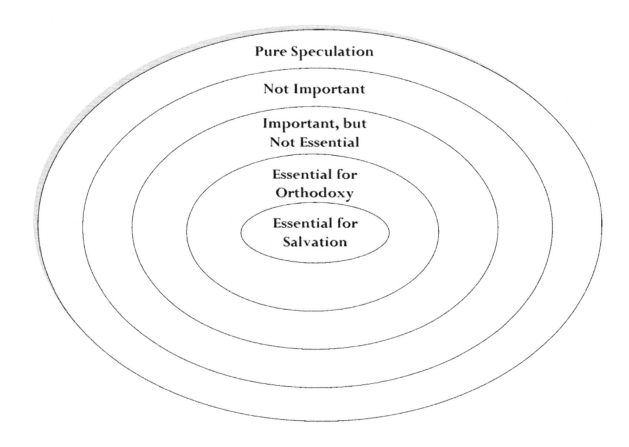

> *"For the Christian, beliefs matter, but not all beliefs matter equally."*
> —Roger Olsen
>
> Mosaic of Christian Beliefs (Downers Grove. IL: IVP. 2002). 33

> *"There are those dogmatic Christians who seem to over define Christianity such that being authentically Christian includes (for them) firm adherence to a detailed set of extrabiblical belief, some of which are quite outside the Great Tradition itself."*
> —Roger Olsen
>
> Mosaic of Christian Beliefs (Downers Grove. IL: IVP. 2002). 33

How certain are you about your beliefs?

"Certain" (Webster's)

- Definite; fixed.
- Sure to come or happen; inevitable.
- Established beyond doubt or question; indisputable.
- Capable of being relied on; dependable.
- Having or showing confidence; assured.

Types of Certainty

1. Emotional Certainty
2. Absolute Certainty
    Mathematical certainty (scientific method)
    Analytical certainty (true by analysis)
3. Intellectual Certainty
    Empirical certainty (weight of evidences)
    Logical certainty (what is reasonable)
4. Moral certainty (what is demanded)

SESSION 6: DEFINING ESSENTIALS AND NON-ESSENTIALS

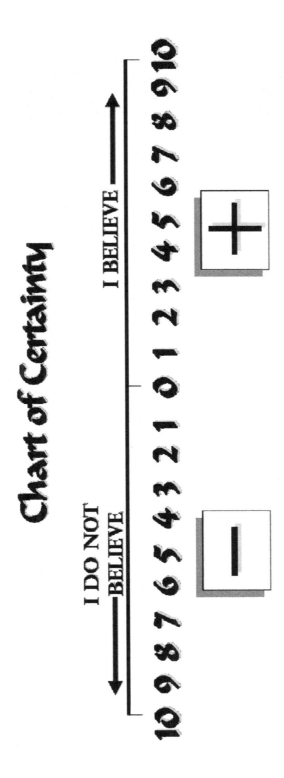

How certain are you that...

Question	Level of Certainty
1. There is a God?	
2. That Christ rose from the grave?	
3. That God loves you?	
4. That Christ is going to come and Rapture the Church before the Great Tribulation?	
5. Christ is coming back to reign on the earth for a thousand years?	
6. That Christ is coming back?	
7. That God wants you to trust that He will protect you from all physical harm?	
8. That God wants you to trust that He will protect you from all emotional harm?	
9. That God wants you to trust in Him in every circumstance?	
10. That the Bible does not have any historical errors?	
11. That Adam and Eve were real people?	
12. That there was really a snake in the garden?	
13. That God created the earth in seven literal days?	
14. The God created the earth?	
15. That Christ paid for the sins of all mankind?	
16. That Christ died for you?	
17. That the Apocrypha (15 books in the Roman Catholic Bible) should not be included in Scripture?	
18. That the book of 3 John should be included in Scripture?	
19. That the book of Genesis should be included in Scripture?	
20. That the gift of tongues ceased in the first century?	

SESSION 6: DEFINING ESSENTIALS AND NON-ESSENTIALS

> "When you overstate, readers will be instantly on guard and everything that has preceded your overstatement as well as everything that follows it will be suspect in their minds because they have lost confidence in your judgment or your poise. Overstatement is one of the common faults. A single overstatement, wherever or however it occurs, diminishes the whole, and a single carefree superlative has the power to destroy, for readers, the object of your enthusiasm."
> —Strunk and White
> *Elements of Style*, (Needham Heights, MA: Allyn and Bacon), 7.

> "In essentials unity, in non-essentials liberty,
> in all things charity."
> —Rupertus Meldenius

Guiding Principles and Application:

1. Don't divide over non-essentials no matter how convicted you are about their truth.

2. Never compromise the essentials no matter what the consequence.

3. There is no shame in being less certain about some things than others. The Bible does not teach all things with the same clarity.

4. Showing honest uncertainty about difficult issues makes your witness more authentic and powerful to a postmodern world.

GROUP DISCUSSION QUESTIONS:

1. Where would you place "getting intoxicated" in the quadrant chart? What is the chief principle that it violates? Are you consistently applying this principle in other parts of your own life? Explain.

2. Many Postmoderns call the Church hypocritical because of inconsistency in what the Church condemns and how Christians live. Explain how someone who does not eat healthy, but who condemns a person for smoking, might be thought of a hypocrite. What can we do to be more consistent?

3. Further discuss which doctrines you believe are essential for salvation. Place them in the center of the Circle of Importance.

SESSION 6: DEFINING ESSENTIALS AND NON-ESSENTIALS

4. Further discuss which doctrines you believe are essential for orthodoxy, other than those you placed in the "essential for salvation" category.

5. Discuss the Chart of Certainty and the answers that you gave to each question.

6. Did your group find essential unity even though you disagree upon minor issues? How does this help you to understand the essential unity of the Body of Christ?

7. How was your thinking most challenged by the lesson? Explain.

Session 7

TRADITIONS IN CHRISTIAN THEOLOGY

Where are your roots?

What is the essential difference in Roman Catholicism, Eastern Orthodoxy, and Protestantism?

Traditions in Christian Theology

1. Roman Catholic

2. Eastern Orthodox

3. Protestant

Protestant	349 million
Roman Catholic	943 million
Orthodox	211 million

> "Justification is the hinge upon which true Christianity stands."
> —John Calvin

> "Christianity stands or falls upon the doctrine of justification."
> —Martin Luther

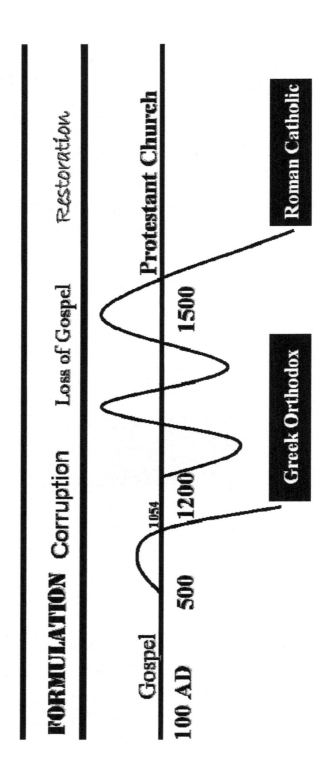

SESSION 7: TRADITIONS IN CHRISTIAN THEOLOGY

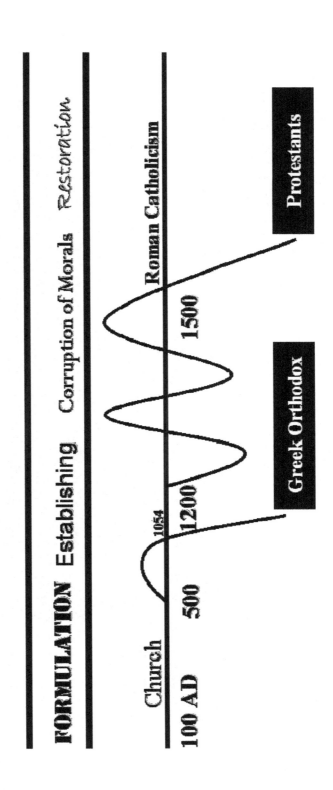

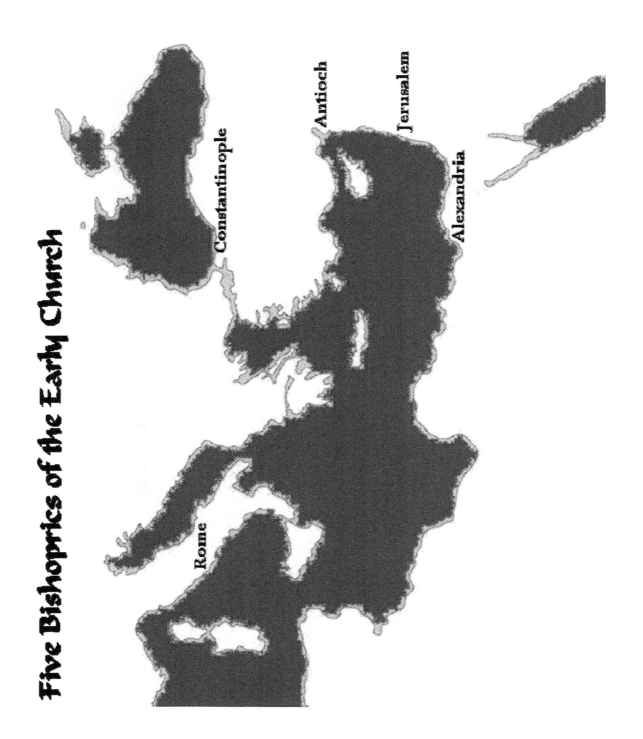

SESSION 7: TRADITIONS IN CHRISTIAN THEOLOGY

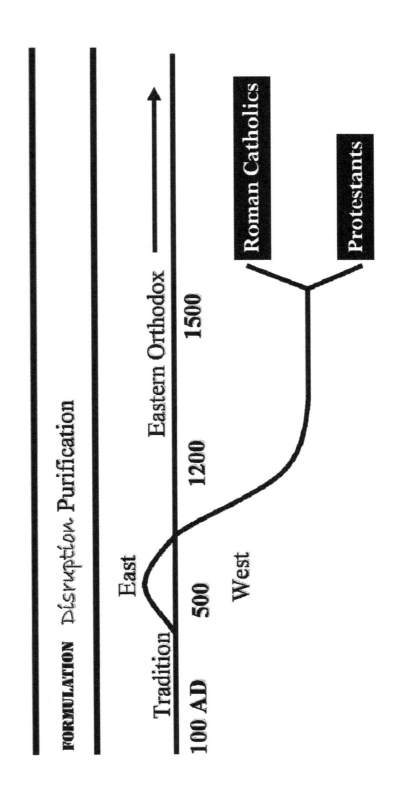

Why are there so many denominations?

Sub-traditions:

- Reformed

- Arminian

- Liberal

- Fundamental

- Charismatic

- Evangelical

- Postmodernist

SESSION 7: TRADITIONS IN CHRISTIAN THEOLOGY

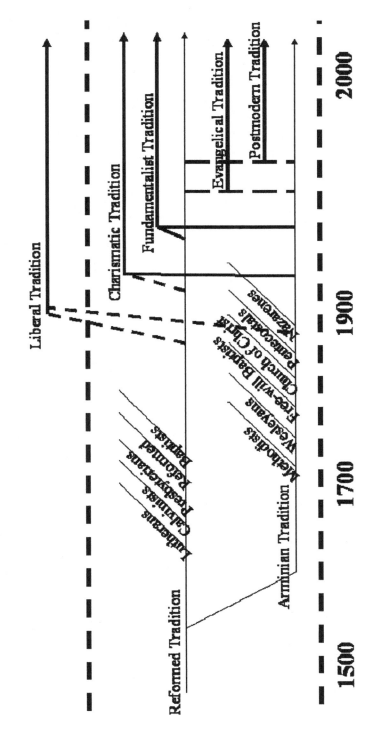

GROUP DISCUSSION QUESTIONS:

1. What confusion or misconceptions have you had in the past concerning division in the Christian Church?

2. Do you agree with the Roman Catholic argument that the Church could not have a canon of the Bible without the authoritative proclamation of the Church? Why or why not?

3. Did this lesson help you understand your own tradition? Explain.

SESSION 7: TRADITIONS IN CHRISTIAN THEOLOGY

4. Why do you think the Protestant Reformers believed that the Gospel was the main essential that determines the true Church? Do you agree? Explain.

5. Do you think the Gospel is preserved in the Protestant Church today? Why or why not?

6. Many are pushing for a "modern reformation." Do you think that the Church is in need of another major reform? Why or why not?

7. Fundamentalism can be used both positively and negatively. Positively, Fundamentalism is the twentieth-century movement that sought to preserve the essentials of Christianity in its fight against liberalism. Negatively, Fundamentalism is thought of as a legalistic sect that, like the Pharisees of Christ's day, places unnecessary burdens on the backs of people. In what ways have you been exposed to Fundamentalism in its negative sense? What can be done to correct this characterization of the Church?

8. Read Matt. 10:34–36. Should the Church continue to be Fundamentalist in the positive sense, even if it divides?

9. How was your thinking most challenged by the lesson? Explain.

Session 8
SOURCES OF THEOLOGY

"Where do we go for truth?"

What are the different sources of truth?

Martin Luther's Trilateral

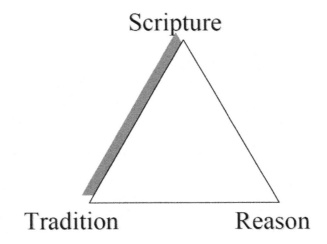

John Wesley's Quadrilateral

Reason	Experience
Tradition	Scripture

1. Tradition

2. Reason

3. Experience

4. General Revelation

5. Emotions

6. Special Revelation (Scripture)

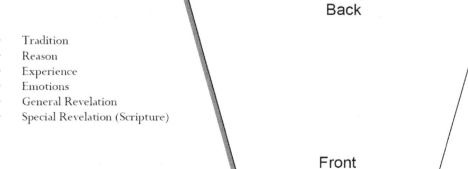

- Tradition
- Reason
- Experience
- Emotions
- General Revelation
- Special Revelation (Scripture)

SESSION 8: SOURCES OF THEOLOGY

ROMAN CATHOLIC STAGE OF TRUTH

Back

Experience

General Revelation
Reason

Tradition   Scripture

Front

EASTERN ORTHODOX STAGE OF TRUTH

Back

General Revelation

Experience
Tradition   Scripture

Front

PROTESTANT REFORMATION STAGE OF TRUTH

Back

- Experience
- General Revelation
- Tradition   Reason
- Scripture

Front

LIBERAL STAGE OF TRUTH

Back

- General Revelation
- Emotions
- Experience
- Reason

Front

SESSION 8: SOURCES OF THEOLOGY

CHARISMATIC STAGE OF TRUTH

Back

**Emotions
Experience
Special Revelation**

Front

FUNDAMENTALIST STAGE OF TRUTH

Back

General Revelation

Scripture

Front

POSTMODERN STAGE OF TRUTH

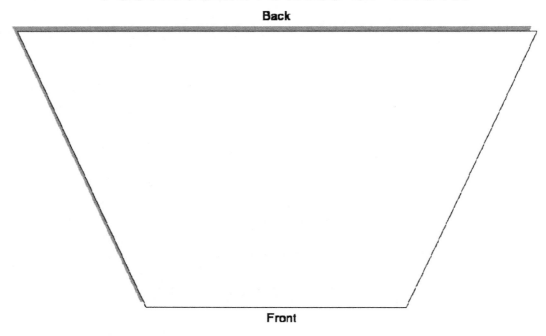

What are the benefits and deficiencies of each source?

Tradition: Religious information that has been handed down to us from various sources.

Examples:

Benefits:

Deficiencies:

SESSION 8: SOURCES OF THEOLOGY

> "Tradition is the living faith of those now dead. Traditionalism is the dead faith of those now living."
> —Jaroslav Pelikan
>
> *The Vindication of Tradition* (New Haven: Yale Univ. Press, 1984), 65

Reason:
Information that comes through the human mind's capacity for logical, rational, and analytic thought.

Examples:

Benefits:

Deficiencies:

> "All truth is given by revelation, either general or special, and it must be received by reason. Reason is the God-given means for discovering the truth that God discloses, whether in his world or his Word. While God wants to reach the heart with truth, he does not bypass the mind."
> —Jonathan Edwards

> "The truth of the Christian faith surpasses the capacity of reason."
>
> —Thomas Aquinas

credo quia absurdum
"I believe because it is absurd"

This Latin phrase coined by Tertullian (150-225) evidences some of the early Church's disdain for the Greek philosophers' reliance upon reason for truth. He said, "What does Athens have to do with Jerusalem, or the academy with the Church?" He sought to return the element of mystery to the Christian faith.

Experience:

Information that comes through direct encounter, participation, or observation.

Examples:

Benefits:

Deficiencies:

SESSION 8: SOURCES OF THEOLOGY

Emotions:
Information that comes through subjectively experienced psychological feelings.

Examples:

Benefits:

Deficiencies:

sensus divinitatus
"Sense of the divine"

> The *sensus divinitatus* is the inward persuasion all people have that directs them to a belief in God and a propensity to worship. While the *sensus divinatas* can contribute to and shape our theology (natural theology), the information is insufficient to bring a person into a right relationship with God.

General Revelation:
Revelation about God given through the created order (Ps 19:1–6; Rom 1:18–20; 2:14–15).

Examples:

Benefits:

Deficiencies:

Special Revelation:

Revelation given by God's supernatural intervention in history through Scripture, miraculous events, divine speech, visible manifestations, etc.

Examples:

Benefits:

Deficiencies:

PROPOSED STAGE OF TRUTH

Back

- Experience
- Emotions
- General Revelation
- Tradition
- Reason
- Scripture

Front

How do the different sources interact to form our theology?

SESSION 8: SOURCES OF THEOLOGY

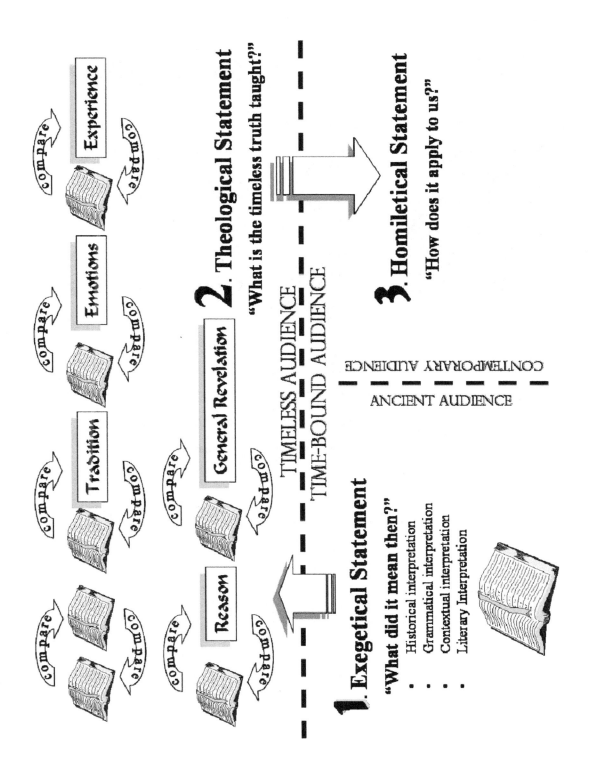

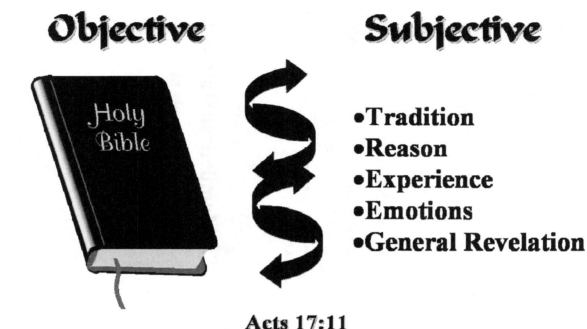

SESSION 8: SOURCES OF THEOLOGY

GROUP DISCUSSION QUESTIONS:

1. Read Rom. 8:28. How has your experience helped you to better understand this passage?

2. Read Rom. 10:13. How has your experience affected the way you read this passage?

3. Read 1 Tim. 2:11–14. How could both your experience and emotions affect the way you interpret this passage? Explain.

4. Tradition is the easiest and most accessible way to acquire information. Further discuss some of the values and dangers of tradition.

5. Sola Scriptura is the reformation principle that Scripture alone is the primary and only infallible source for truth. In what ways do we deny this principle in our own lives? What can be done to correct this?

6. What have you learned about God from General Revelation?

SESSION 8: SOURCES OF THEOLOGY

7. How can you have a respect for tradition while at the same time avoiding traditionalism?

8. Which stage of truth do you aspire to, and which stage of truth do you actually live according to? How can you correct this?

9. How was your thinking most challenged by the lesson? Explain.

Session 9

EXCURSES: DOES GOD STILL SPEAK TODAY?

Should we seek out a prophet?

Has Special Revelation ceased, or does God still communicate to people through prophets, dreams, visions, and audible encounters?

Three positions:

1. Continuationism

2. Hard Cessationism

3. Soft Cessationism

Temporary Gifts		Permanent Gifts	
Supernatural Sign		Speaking	Serving
Revelatory	Confirmatory		
• Apostleship • Prophecy • Discerning of spirits • Word of wisdom • Word of knowledge • Tongues • Interpretation of tongues	• Healings • Miracles • Tongues	• Evangelism • Teaching • Pastor-teacher • Exhortation	• Service • Showing Mercy • Giving • Administrations • Helps

What is the Continuationist view of Prophecy?

Continuationism: The view that miraculous sign gifts are still being given and, therefore, God still speaks directly in various ways today.

Adherents: Wayne Grudem, Jack Deere, Craig Keener, Jack Hayford, John Piper, J.P. Moreland

Defense of Continuationism:

1. Acts 2:14-21 seems to teach that supernatural occurrences such as tongues and prophecy would be normative for the Church era.

2. The entire book of Acts seems to show that the supernatural gifts are common within the Church.

3. All of Scripture supports the idea that it is God's nature to work in supernatural ways.

4. The New Testament never explicitly states that the supernatural sign gifts would cease.

> *"If you were to lock a brand-new Christian in a room with a Bible and tell him to study what Scripture has to say about healings and miracles, he would never come out of the room a cessationist."*
>
> —Jack Deere
>
> _{Surprised by the Power of the Spirit (Grand Rapids, MI: Zondervan, 1997), 54}

What is the Hard Cessationist view of Prophecy?

Hard Cessationism: The view that miraculous sign gifts ceased with the death of the last apostle and the completion of the New Testament. Therefore, God does not speak directly to people today.

Adherents: Charles Hodge, Charles Ryrie, John MacArthur, majority of Church history

Defense of Hard Cessationism:

1. The Bible implicitly supports the idea that the supernatural sign gifts were for the establishment of the Church era.

Eph. 2:19-20
"So then you are no longer foreigners and noncitizens, but you are fellow citizens with the saints and members of God's household, because you have been built on the foundation of the apostles and prophets, with Christ Jesus himself as the cornerstone."

2 Cor. 12:12
"Indeed, the signs of an apostle were performed among you with great perseverance by signs and wonders and powerful deeds."

Heb. 2:3-4
"How will we escape if we neglect such a great salvation? It was first communicated through the Lord and was confirmed to us by those who heard him, while God confirmed their witness with signs and wonders and various miracles and gifts of the Holy Spirit distributed according to his will."

1 Cor. 13:8-10
"Love never ends. But if there are prophecies, they will be set aside; if there are tongues, they will cease; if there is knowledge, it will be set aside. For we know in part and we prophesy in part; but when the perfect comes, the partial will be done away."

2. It is agreed that the Bible never explicitly states that the sign gifts have ceased. But the Bible never explicitly states that Scripture is complete, yet both cessationists and non-cessationists agree that it is.

3. If God is still speaking supernaturally through prophecy, tongues, word of wisdom, etc., then the Canon of Scripture is still open.

> "It might, indeed, be *a priori* conceivable that God should deal with men [individually], and reveal Himself and His will to each individual, throughout the whole course of history, in the [depths] of his own consciousness. This is the mystics dream. It has not, however, been God's way. He has chosen rather to deal with the race in its entirety, and to give this race His complete revelation of Himself in an organic whole."
> —B.B. Warfield
>
> *Counterfeit Miracles* (Carlisle, PN: Banner of Truth, 1972), 26

4. If one were to examine the Scripture closely, it becomes evident that God's direct intervention through prophecy and supernatural signs and wonders was not the norm as it may seem. The Bible, as theological history (not exhaustive history), only records the times when God does intervene, thereby giving the impression that God's direct encounters through prophets, dreams, visions, etc. are God's modus operandi when they are not.

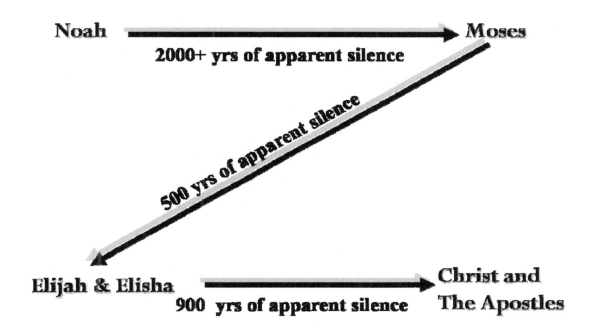

5. History convincingly suggests that the supernatural sign gifts have ceased. We do not see evidence of confirmed prophets after the death of the last apostle. Only fringe groups here and there have claimed that God still speaks through prophets, tongues, etc., until the twentieth century when the charismatic revival began.

> "This whole place [1 Cor. 12 on spiritual gifts] is very obscure . . . but the obscurity is produced by our ignorance of the facts referred to and by their cessation, being such as then used to occur, but now no longer take place."
> —John Chrysostom (347-407)
> ECF 2.12.1.1.29.0

> "In the earliest time the Holy Ghost fell upon them that believed: and they spoke with tongues which they had not learned 'as the Spirit gave them utterance.' These were signs adapted to the time. For it was proper for the Holy Spirit to evidence Himself in all tongues, and to show that the Gospel of God had come to all tongues [languages] over the whole earth. The thing was done for a authentication and it passed away."
> —St. Augustine (354-430)
> Ten Homilies on the first Epistle of John VI, 10

What is the Soft Cessationist view of Prophecy?

Soft Cessationism: Or "Soft Continuationist." The view that the miraculous sign gifts could still be given today, but believers need to be careful about outright acceptance of people's claims of possession.

Adherents: D. A. Carson, Robert Saucy, Millard Erickson

SESSION 9: EXCURSES: DOES GOD STILL SPEAK TODAY?

Defense of Soft Cessationism:

1. Neither side's arguments are conclusive. We must therefore proceed with great caution.

2. While it may be true that Church history has not seen the continuation of God speaking directly, this does not mean that it is not possible.

> "God, in his ordinary providence, makes use of means, yet is free to work without, above, and against them, at his pleasure."
> —Westminster Confession of Faith
> 5.3

3. Those who adhere to a futuristic interpretation of Revelation must concede that there are going to be prophets in the future as represented by the Two Witnesses (Rev. 11:3) and, possibly, the 144,000 Israelites (Rev. 7:4). Therefore, we must be open to further direct revelation from God.

Guiding Principles:

- God's Word is not something to be trifled with (Ex. 20:7).

- If you are a prophet, you must show convincing signs of a prophet (Deut 18:15-22).

- If you are a prophet, you must have orthodox theology (Deut. 13:1-3).

- If someone believes that they have a word from the Lord, they had better be certain and be ready to live by the consequences if it turns out false.

GROUP DISCUSSION QUESTIONS:

1. In what ways have you experienced what you thought might be the "voice of God," either through experience or emotion? How certain can you be that it was in fact God's voice?

2. Many people become more desirous to hear the "voice of God" outside of Scripture when there are difficulties in their lives. What is the danger in this? Explain.

3. How have you been mislead by what you thought was God's voice? In what ways did this confuse you?

SESSION 9: EXCURSES: DOES GOD STILL SPEAK TODAY? 131

4. Hard cessationists have been falsely accused of denying that God can work miracles today, when in reality they do not deny that God can work miracles, but that God gifts particular people to work miracles. A hard cessationist may pray for God to miraculously heal someone of cancer just as hopefully as a continuationist. Does this clear up some misunderstanding? Explain.

5. A verified prophet is one who performs an incredible sign or wonder, leaving no doubt in the minds of the observer that he or she is a prophet. Have you ever witnessed this? Explain.

6. God speaks in many different ways. The argument of this lesson is that we cannot be certain that we are hearing "God's voice" unless it is verified through rightly interpreted Scripture or a verified prophet. How important does this make our study of Scripture? Explain.

7. How do you often "put God in a box" in your own life? Explain.

8. How was your thinking most challenged by the lesson? Explain.

Session 10

UNITY AND DIVERSITY

Doing Theology in the Emerging Context

What is Unity?

> John 17:22-23
>
> "The glory you gave to me I have given to them, that they may be one just as we are one—I in them and you in me—that they may be completely one, so that the world will know that you sent me, and you have loved them just as you have loved me."

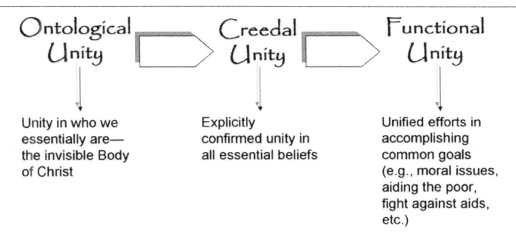

Ontological Unity	Creedal Unity	Functional Unity
Unity in who we essentially are—the invisible Body of Christ	Explicitly confirmed unity in all essential beliefs	Unified efforts in accomplishing common goals (e.g., moral issues, aiding the poor, fight against aids, etc.)

Apostles Creed

I believe in God the Father, Almighty, Maker of heaven and earth
And in Jesus Christ, his only begotten Son, our Lord
Who was conceived by the Holy Ghost, born of the Virgin Mary
Suffered under Pontius Pilate; was crucified, dead and buried; He descended into hell
The third day he rose again from the dead
He ascended into heaven, and sits at the right hand of God the Father Almighty
From thence he shall come to judge the quick and the dead
I believe in the Holy Ghost
I believe a holy catholic church; the communion of saints
The forgiveness of sins
The resurrection of the body
And the life everlasting. Amen.

Unity and Diversity among the Traditions

Doctrine of Man and Grace
(fifth century)

Doctrine of Christ
Definition of Chalcedon (+51)

Trinity (325)
Counsel of Nicea (325)

Doctrine of the Atonement
(eleventh century)

100 A.D.   400 A.D.   1100 A.D.   1600 A.D.   2000 A.D.

Unity and Diversity among Protestant Denominations

Five "Solas" of the Protestant Reformation

Reformed Understanding	Sola Scriptura	Solus Christus	Sola Gratia	Sola Fide	Soli deo Gloria
Meaning	The "Scripture alone" contains primary authority to dictate the lives of believers.	The work of "Christ alone" is the basis for justification.	Justification is by means of God's "grace alone."	"Faith alone" is the only instrumental cause of justification.	All is done for "God's glory alone."

SESSION 10: UNITY AND DIVERSITY

```
                                    Doctrine of Scripture
            Doctrine of Man and Grace (sixteenth century)
                (fifth century)
                                    Doctrine of Justification
            Doctrine of Christ      (sixteenth century)
            Definition of Chalcedon (451)
      Trinity           Doctrine of the Atonement
      Counsel of Nicea (325)  (eleventh century)
  ──────────────────────────────────────────────────────▶
  100 A.D.   400 A.D.   1100 A.D.   1600 A.D.   2000 A.D.
```

Unity and Diversity among the Sexes

Unity and Diversity among the Nations

Luke 8:5-18

GROUP DISCUSSION QUESTIONS:

1. How does the concept of Unity and Diversity help you to better understand the Church today?

2. Why is it that we have required Introduction to Theology as a prerequisite to all other courses?

3. Briefly outline the proposed method that this course has suggested for "doing theology."

4. What is the advantage of doing theology this way?

5. What is the risk involved and is it worth is? Explain.

6. What ways has this class caused you to do theology differently? Be specific.

7. Concerning the Parable of the Soils, give examples when you have failed to believe or apply God's word to your life and you moved further away from God as a result. What can you do to avoid this?

8. What is the most significant thing that you have learned in this class that has made you change the way you think?

Appendix:
REPRESENTING CHRIST TO A POSTMODERN WORLD

A Peanuts cartoon depicted a conversation between Linus and Charlie Brown. Charlie Brown was confused and disillusioned by his failing beliefs when Linus comforted him with these timely words: "It doesn't matter what you believe as long as you are sincere." I also recently heard a religious leader on television state that if the bones of Christ were to be discovered in Palestine today, this would not alter his Christian faith; his faith was not bound by objective truths.

Surveys are becoming emphatically more clear that the majority of our culture believes that truth is relative.[1] It has been clear for some time now that our world is going through a major cultural shift. The illustrations stated above are all too common in today's postmodern[2] society. We have moved from a world of absolutes, objectivity, and dogmatism to one of relativism, subjectivism, and tolerance. The greatest commandment in this postmodern society is this, THOU SHALT TOLERATE ONE ANOTHER. Springing forth from this relativistic epistemology,[3] tolerance has become preeminent. As one writer has put it, "Tolerance has become so important that no exception is tolerated."[4] A person may have his or her religion, and may believe it, but he or she has no right to try to persuade another of his or her belief. Why?

---

[1] Subjective, pluralistic, and pragmatic also accurately describe our culture, but for this study we will primarily use the term relative and its cognates assuming a tight relationship between all the terms.

[2] This term will be further defined as we proceed in our study. Most briefly, "postmodern" describes a current trend within our culture that began in the late 20th century that is relativistic in its thinking concerning truth and knowledge.

[3] Epistemology describes the way we understand the nature and grounds of knowledge.

[4] Charles Colson, *How Now Shall We Live* (Wheaton, IL: Tyndale, 1999) p. 23.

Because what you are saying is that your belief is superior to their belief. This is the supreme act of intolerance, the primary postmodern taboo.

It is not my purpose here to outline and detail the rise of postmodernism as many others have sufficiently done.[1] Neither is it my purpose to critique postmodernism as a movement. What I shall attempt to do is to give the Christian some practical direction on how to represent Christ in a postmodern world.

I shall deal with three primary issues with which the Christian needs to wrestle. The first of these is the issue of tolerance. This is the question: How are we to react to a culture whose battle cry is tolerance? Are we to join in? Does the Bible have anything to say about whether we are to tolerate each other and in what ways? Secondly, we need to briefly and practically tackle the postmodern idea that all truth is relative. Many churches are joining hands with our culture and embracing this view of relativity. Others compensate by rejecting any notion of relative truth whatsoever, claiming that all truth is objective. What does the Bible have to say about truth and relativity? Are there truths that are relative as the postmodern claims? Or is all truth absolute and objective? And third, among the truths that are objective (assuming that there is objective truth), what are the essentials and non-essentials? The early Church during the Diocletian persecutions (AD 302-305) was forced to begin to define the canon of Scripture.[2] The Romans were arresting and killing Christians who possessed Scriptures. Nobody wanted to give up his life for a book that was not inspired; it was not worth dying for. In our postmodern age, it is more important than ever to define

---

1 See Millard Erickson, *Truth or Consequences* (Downers Grove, IL: IVP, 2001); Douglas Groothuis, *Truth Decay* (Downers Grove, IL: IVP, 2000); J. Grenz, *A Primer on Postmodernism* (Grand Rapids, MI: Eerdmans, 1996); J. Richard Middleton & Brian J. Walsh, *Truth is Stronger Than it Used To Be* (Downers Grove, IL: Intervarsity Press, 1995). Also see Walter Truitt Anderson, *Reality Isn't What it Used to Be* (San Francisco, CA: Harper Collins, 1990).

2 John Hannah, *Our Legacy* (Colorado Springs, CO: NavPress, 2001) p. 41.

what truths are worth dying for. We need to be able to distinguish between what is essential for the Christian faith and what is non-essential.

Christian Tolerance?

Often when false claims are promoted, the reaction is to defend the truth by going to the opposite extreme. The early church, when battling with Pelagius' false view of anthropology, in order to defend the doctrine of depravity (as they should have done), went to the opposite extreme and promoted the doctrines of purgatory and limbo to account for the children who, although depraved, could not exercise faith.[1] Many Calvinists in the 17th century countered the Arminians by emphasizing God's sovereignty to such an extent that they seemed to support the idea that God was the author of sin and evil. Often times it is human nature to counter false beliefs by promoting equally false beliefs of the opposite extreme. If you don't believe me, just think to the last argument you had with your spouse where he or she told you that you were overreacting to a situation. You respond by stating that you were NOT overreacting and that you NEVER overreact. It may have been true that you were not overreacting in that instance, but it is probably not true that you NEVER overreact. In order to prove what you believe to be a false statement to be false ("you are overreacting"), you offer an equally false statement in its place ("you NEVER overreact"). It is the classic pendulum effect. We all do this in many ways. But tragically, today this is often the result when Christians counter a postmodern relativistic epistemology. When we hear that the culture is stating that there are no absolute truths, it is our tendency to clinch our fists and promote objectivity at all costs. When we find that tolerance has become the most important virtue of a

---

[1] See Jacques Le Goff, *The Birth of Purgatory* (Chicago: University of Chicago, 1984) who states that Augustine was the "true father of purgatory" (p. 61).

godless society, it is our tendency to throw out tolerance all together.[1] But what does the Bible have to say about tolerance? Are we to tolerate each other?

This question must be asked more exactly before its answer can benefit our present study. Two different groups of people need to be in focus: (1) those who are part of the body of Christ (the Church) and believe in absolute truth[2] and (2) those who are outside the body of Christ and have bought into the postmodern fad of relativity. There is a difference between asking "Are we to tolerate the sin of a Christian?" and "Are we to tolerate the sin of a non-Christian?" We will meet the challenge of the non-Christian first; then we will move on to the Christian.

Tolerance of those outside the Church

Practically speaking, the only truth that the postmodern believes is that there is no truth, or at least no objective access to that truth. We are all confined to our own ideas of what is right or wrong, true or false. But whatever our conclusions may be, they are merely our opinions, and our opinions are no better than those of another. Therefore, to the postmodern, all of us are imprisoned behind the unbreakable walls of this subjective reality, and therefore we must all "tolerate" each other. It is not uncommon to hear statements like this: "If you believe that the Bible is God's Word, that is fine and good, but you must also tolerate the person who believes in the Quran or any other religious literature they may choose." But here is where the problem arises: What do the postmoderns mean by "tolerate"? Do they

---

[1] Please understand that I am not demoting the Christian's need to stand for truth. Christianity is not a religion that can exist without the doctrine of absolute truth. I commend many within the Church today who have been equipping Christians to stand up for absolute truth. I am simply attempting to place a buffer between the extremes so that we can stay faithful to the truth of Scripture in a relevant way.

[2] I am not implying that all Christians believe in absolute truth. In fact, I believe that there are a lot who don't. In my ministry to single adults, both young and old, I am having my eyes opened to the truth of Stanley Toussaint, a former professor of mine at Dallas Seminary, who taught me that "the sins of the culture become the sins of the Church." The postmodern philosophy of the culture is beginning to flood our pews.

mean that we are simply to live together without killing each other? Do they mean the same as the American Heritage Dictionary's definition of what it means to tolerate: "To allow without prohibiting or opposing; permit"? Do they simply mean that if I have a neighbor who adheres to a belief system other than mine that I am supposed to live at peace with him, not prohibiting or oppressing him? If this is the case, I agree. I am "tolerant" and should be. I concede that, at least in this case, the postmodern objective is good because I do not have the authority or power to prohibit anyone from believing whatever they choose. If this is the case, then all is well.

But in reality, this is not what typical postmoderns mean when they cry for "tolerance." They are not asking people to simply tolerate and get along with the opposing belief. The fact is that they are asking people to compromise their beliefs. They are asking me to concede that my neighbor's beliefs are just as true as mine, to forfeit my notion of objectivity, and to surrender my view of exclusivism. The result would accomplish nothing less than to render a death blow to my belief in the Scriptures. What they are implying when they push their definition of "tolerance" is that people should never stand up for their beliefs, if standing up for them means stating that their beliefs are the only true beliefs—that they are exclusive. They are not asking people to tolerate the homosexual, but to change their belief that homosexuality is wrong for everyone. But, again, this is not asking someone to be tolerant; it is asking someone to compromise his or her beliefs and convert to the postmodern faith. This is something that the Christian cannot do.

Christians should join hands with the postmodern in this cry for tolerance if tolerance means that we live at peace with those of other faiths, not prohibiting them from believing something unbiblical—that is God's job. But, of course, this is not what they are asking. By tolerance, the postmodern means that we compromise the objectivity of God's Word. By tolerance, the postmodern cries for us to stop reaching out to others with the Gospel. By tolerance, the postmodern demands that we approve of their lifestyles. By tolerance, the postmodern is essentially asking us to give up our faith. This we cannot do.

The first step in understanding and reaching out to the postmodern non-Christian is for us all to be able to understand and compellingly argue that it is not tolerance that they want, but compromise.

Tolerance of those Within the Church

As I stated earlier, it is important for us to separate what it means for us to be tolerant to those outside the Church from what it means to be tolerant to those within the Church. We have already concluded that we are to tolerate those outside the Church, as long as tolerance means that we live at peace with those of different beliefs than ours. But how is it different within the Church? Does the Bible have anything to say about tolerance among believers?

The answer is "yes." In chapter four of his epistle to the Ephesians, Paul begins to tell his readers how they are to live the Christian life. Speaking on the importance of unity, Paul states, "Therefore, I, the prisoner of the Lord, implore you to walk in a manner worthy of the calling with which you have been called, with all humility and gentleness, with patience, *showing tolerance for one another in love*, being diligent to preserve the unity of the Spirit in the bond of peace" (Eph. 4:1-3, emphasis added). Here Paul tells us that one of the primary ways the Church preserves unity is by showing tolerance. The participle avnecomenoi here has the meaning "to endure, bear with, to put up with."12 The King James often translates it, "to suffer with." This word is used by Christ when He cries over Israel, "how long shall I put up with you" (Matt 17:17, emphasis added). It almost always carries a negative connotation. In 2 Maccabees 9:12, it is used of an unbearable stench; the smell was said to be intolerable. In his letter to the Ephesians, Paul is telling the Church that it will sometimes be necessary to tolerate the "stench" of one another. This presupposes something negative about the ones we are to tolerate. Someone may have a repulsive personality—Paul tells us to endure them! Another has a bad temper—bear with them! Someone differs with you in some non-essential doctrine—tolerate them! Let's face it, when we all get to heaven we will all find out that we were wrong about a few things. Some more than others, but we will all have some surprises.

So, the question is not whether we, as Christians, are to show tolerance to fellow believers, but to what extent are we to be tolerant? Is there a difference in tolerating a Christian who smokes a pipe and tolerating a Christian who is involved in a homosexual relationship? Should we distinguish between tolerating one who is a non-cessationist and one who denies the Trinity? These are the issues that will inevitably arise when discussing the issue of tolerance in a postmodern society. The first thing that we, as Christians, need to establish is that some type of tolerance is mandated in Scripture. We will shortly decide what this tolerance looks like and how it plays out.

Christian Relativism?

Before we can begin to define the ways in which Christians are to be tolerant, we must first fit another piece into the puzzle. This piece is the issue of relativism. Again, relativism is at the heart of the postmodern epistemology. It is not uncommon to hear one say, "Christ is my way to God, but I don't push my beliefs on others." Or, "Western Christianity has no right to push its beliefs on others who are perfectly comfortable with their religion and have been for hundreds of years." Relativism is the idea that truth is contained only in the eye of the beholder. Like the Peanuts cartoon I referred to earlier, "It doesn't matter what you believe as long as you are sincere." To the relative postmodern, all truth is contingent upon the situation, culture, or language of the person. With relativism, a moral truth can be true and binding for one person, while for another it is not. Having an abortion may be wrong for one person and right for another. Likewise, the true relativistic postmodern may claim that two conflicting statements can both be true at the same time. For example, one may claim that Jesus Christ is the Son of God and another could claim that He is not the Son of God. To the postmodern, both of these statements could be true at the same time. The law of non-contradiction is not binding to the relativist. A new law has taken its place, the law of relativism.

This proposal from the postmodern that all truth is relative has again caused the Church to be on the defensive. The tendency for the Christian is to fight absolute relativism with the opposite extreme, absolute objectivism. Absolute objectivism believes that all truths are objective in the same way absolute relativism believes that all truths are relative. Objective truths are just the opposite of relative truths. They do not depend upon the situation, culture, language, or any other variable. Objective truths are truths that exist in and of themselves. They are true even if nobody believes them to be true. An example of an objective truth may be the fact that I have daughters named Katelynn and Kylee or that the sun shines. These are truths that exist independently. They do not need anything to affirm them in order for them to be true. As Christians we emphatically affirm the existence of objective truths. It is one of the bedrocks of Christianity. It is because of the objective truth of the atonement that you and I can have access to God. It is because of the objective truth that God created us that we exist. There is no room for relativity in these matters. It is our job to defend many of these objective truths at all costs. But this is usually where we, and our extremist nature, often take things too far. While it is our job to defend certain truths at all costs, it is not our job to defend all truth at all costs. In order to counter the one who believes that all truth is relative, we may state that all truth is objective. But is that true? Is all truth objective?

Paul, writing to the Romans, deals with a situation that is relevant to our question. Young believers were often convinced that it was wrong to eat foods that were considered unclean. Paul emphatically states that all foods were clean: "I know and am convinced in the Lord Jesus that nothing is unclean in itself" (Rom. 14:14a). Paul was saying that it was OK to eat ham! This is the objective truth, right? Not quite. The objective reality was that all foods were clean, but there was a relative situation which determined whether or not it was right or wrong to eat these foods: "But to him who thinks anything to be unclean, to him it is unclean" (14:14b). Therefore, if someone thought that it was a sin to eat ham, but did it anyway, this was a sin to him. Not because God would be angry that the person ate what was unclean, but because he consciously believed it was wrong and therefore rebelled against his conscience and God. Not only this, but Paul goes on to state that whatever is done without full conviction that it is right is sin (v. 23). This means that if I believe that wearing brown slippers is a sin, but I do it anyway, it becomes sin for me. Not that wearing brown slippers is wrong, but because I am in conscious rebellion against God. Likewise, if I believe that listening to a certain type of music on the radio is wrong but I do it anyway, to me this is wrong. But while it is wrong for me, it may not be wrong for the person in the passenger seat next to me who has no conviction whatsoever that it is wrong. In this situation, the postmodern is correct—the truth, right or wrong, is relative. It is relative upon whether or not the person was acting against their conscience. For one person it was wrong to listen to the music, for the other it was not. For one person it may have been wrong to eat ham, for another it was not. There are many other situations like that just described which occur in our lives everyday. The point that I am trying to make is that truth is sometimes relative. We as Christians need to realize this if we are to speak intelligently to a postmodern world.

But how does one tell which truths are relative and which are objective? It is not always easy. There are some things that are not clearly spoken of as right or wrong in Scripture. Therefore, the person must prayerfully revert to his or her own conscience for guidance. But the reality is that the Scriptures speak truthfully and objectively in the principles that they cover. All Christians are subject to the truth of God's Word—no exceptions.

Emphasizing the Essentials

Now we return to the question of tolerance within the Church. To what extent are we to tolerate the objective sinful behavior of a believer? What beliefs are the sine qua non (without which, not) of the true Christian? In other words, bare minimum, what does a person have to believe to be saved? This is one of the most important exercises that we can endeavor to accomplish in representing Christ to a postmodern world. We must recognize the difference between the essentials of the Christian faith and the non-essentials. Concerning salvation, we need to be able to state exactly what the Bible says is essential for salvation — what exactly is the content of what a person needs to believe to be saved. Does one simply have to "believe in the Lord Jesus" (Acts 16:31)? If so what does that entail? What does one have to know about Christ? Does he have to know that He is God? Does he have to believe that Christ vicariously took his place on the cross? Does he have to believe and turn from his sin? Or does he just have to believe, as the thief on the cross did, that Christ was the messianic King going to His Kingdom? What about the Holy Spirit? Must one believe in Him before he or she is born again? Do you have to believe in the Trinity, the virgin birth, the inspiration of Scripture, the Second Coming of Christ, or the existence of Hell? The list could go on and on. The question is this: Are these all doctrines that the unbeliever must accept before he or she is considered a believer? There is not time here to fully exhaust this vital study. I apologize, but it is not my intention to define exactly the essentials for salvation.[1] There are many, even within evangelicalism, who disagree as to what exactly is essential and what is not. My intention is to put forth the relevancy of this subject. It is extremely important that we categorize just exactly what the Bible says about salvation.

Likewise, it is also important for us to determine what is essential for sanctification. Is it essential that people hold to the correct eschatology (understanding of the future things) for them to grow in Christ-likeness? If so, how important is it? Is it essential that a believer be baptized? How essential is it if a believer continually neglects to share the Gospel? This list could also go on and on. And again, it is not my purpose to bring you to a conclusion on these matters. It is my purpose, however, to help you to understand the importance of struggling with these issues and to have a grid through which to filter them. It is to this we now turn.

Take a look at the attached quadrant chart. It is a key to understanding what we are talking about. I have found it to be very useful in many situations. It is very simple, yet extremely helpful in creating a mental grid through which one can filter many of these issues. It has two broad categories, each divided into two sections. Following are the category definitions. Observe the patterns on the chart as you read.

1. **True Relativity**: Everything that exists on the left side of the quadrant is truly relative. It is either completely independent of right or wrong, or the right or wrong is determined by the situation.

> a. *Situational Relativity*: The right and the wrong of those in this category are dependent upon the culture, time, situation, or some other variable. Women

---

[1] Although it seems clear that the most vital of all the essentials is the death, burial, and resurrection of Christ. Paul seems to have made that abundantly clear in 1 Corinthians 15, "For I delivered to you as of *first importance* what I also received, that Christ died for our sins according to the Scriptures, and that He was buried, and that He was raised on the third day according to the Scriptures" (1 Cor 15:3-4, emphasis added).

not wearing a head covering (1 Cor. 11:5) is a good example. While the women who did not wear a head covering were expressing an underlying sinful principle, the wearing of the head covering itself was not right or wrong. Its sinfulness was dependent upon the cultural expression. The same sin may be expressed in our culture but in a different way.

b. *Autonomous Relativity*: This category contains those that are truly relative. There is no right or wrong. This category is filled primarily with opinions and autonomous customs that are not related to right or wrong. One's opinion on the best song is an example of something that is autonomously relative. There is no one correct answer that exists by itself — it is always relative.

2. **True Objectivity**: All that is on the right side of the quadrant is the objective side. Everything on this side has a definite right or wrong. There is always an objective truth that is true no matter whether one believes it. It is not dependent upon time, culture, or any situation. It exists as true or false in and of itself. All biblical principles and doctrines belong on this side.

a. *Essential Objectivity*: In our current chart, this category contains only those that are essential for salvation.[1] This should contain only those truths which you believe a person must accept to be considered a true Christian.

b. *Non-Essential Objectivity*: This category contains both doctrinal and nondoctrinal issues which are not necessary for one's salvation. A good example might be whether one believes in the cessation of the gift of tongues. Tongues either ceased or they did not cease. The truth is objective. But at the same time, it is non-essential because it is not necessary to believe one way or the other as a prerequisite to salvation.

---

1 This quadrant could also be used for the things that are essential for sanctification.

APPENDIX

Read the categories carefully. After you have finished, construct your own chart. Keep it with you for a few weeks. When issues arise, decide the category in which you think they belong. Be critical of yourself. This chart is extremely valuable in understanding that these categories exist. It is not an ironclad never-fail chart that you can use in all situations. In fact, your chart will probably look different from mine in some areas. The value of this chart is to express the necessity of thinking about these areas more deeply. We live in a postmodern culture in which people live their lives on the left side of the quadrant (relativism). We have a Church that wants to counter by living on the right side (objectivism). By becoming familiar with the principles of this chart, we will be able to express truth in a more relevant fashion.

Another key value of this chart is to better place emphasis where emphasis is due. Many Christians overly stress their views (many of which are relative) on certain issues to an unbelieving postmodern, giving them the wrong impression. We express our opinions about having a glass of wine, rock-and-roll or some other area just as emphatically as we would the death, burial, and resurrection of Christ. We do so as if we believe that convincing someone that rock-and-roll is wrong is the same as convincing them of the Gospel. We must understand that convincing someone of any area outside of the objective essential will not save them. That is a big problem within the Church — we major in the minors. We will argue all day long with the unbeliever about the theory of evolution and never tell them about Christ. We never even give them a chance to believe what is most important. Let me make this clear: There is nothing wrong with discussing or even debating the non-essentials, but we must keep in mind that the non-essentials do not save. They can be used as primers and springboards for the Gospel, but they cannot replace it. We must get to the Gospel in every witnessing opportunity we have. Eleven of the twelve sermons in Acts contain the death, burial, and resurrection of Christ. The only one that did not was Stephen's, and if it were not cut short, he surely would have presented the risen Christ to the Sanhedrin. It is imperative that we emphasize the Gospel; it is the only message that contains eternal life.

> Look *and* see what the matter with this paragraph is. It is *taught* in writing class that *you* do not emphasize *too many* words. You save *your* emphasis for *times* that *really* matter. If you *emphasize* too much, then when you come to a *word* or a *statement* that you really want to stress, *you have no stronger way to express your emphasis. All* the emphases *will* look as if they carry the *same* importance.

This is precisely what the Church does with many issues and doctrines. We may emphasize some non-essential so much that when we come to the things that are really important, we have no more *stress* left—it is *called overstatement.* Strunk and White, in their excellent book on writing, *The Elements of Style*, warn concerning overstatement:

> "When you overstate, readers will be instantly on guard and everything that has preceded your overstatement as well as everything that follows it will be suspect in their minds because they have lost confidence in your judgment or your poise. Overstatement is one of the common faults. A single overstatement, wherever or however it occurs, diminishes the whole, and a single carefree superlative has the power to destroy, for readers, the object of your enthusiasm."[1]

---
1 Strunk and White, *Elements of Style*, (Needham Heights, MA: Allyn and Bacon), 7.

If too much emphasis is placed on the non-essentials, this does not make the non-essentials more important, but it makes the essentials less important. We end up destroying the "object of our enthusiasm"— the Gospel of Christ. Once this happens, the unbelieving postmodern may then accept the essentials only because they have taken on a lower status of relativity. We have to continually ask ourselves what things we have placed in italics in our lives and if they deserve to be there. Most people's lives are filled with opinions, pet peeves, disputes, and hang-ups. When the unbelieving postmodern looks at you, what would he say that you have in italics in your life? We should have very few things that we greatly emphasize in order to save our stress for the things that really matter. We can give no greater honor to Christ than to emphasize the things that He emphasized.

Conclusion

Can we tolerate the postmodern? What are the issues which we are to tolerate? These are questions that have not yet been fully answered. Tolerance is a difficult issue, and interrogation of some of the more specific issues must be postponed for now. It is my prayer that interest in learning and teaching the essential fundamentals of the Faith has been stirred within. Progress has been made. We understand that tolerance is a mandate within the Church. We also understand that the Bible teaches that there are many situations in which truth is relative. These steps are vital to our witness to a postmodern culture. If we are to evangelize in the world today, we need to be relevant. We do not panic when someone says that truth is relative, we explain that they are right, but only some truth is relative. When they cry for tolerance, we cry with them, and explain to them the difference between tolerance and compromise.

Having done this, it is important to remember that we, as believers, will still be rejected. As Christ said, "Remember the word that I said to you, 'A slave is not greater than his master.' If they persecuted Me, they will also persecute you…" (John 15:20). What we, as Christians, need to make sure of is that we are being persecuted for the right thing. We do not want to give the unbeliever any more reason for rejecting Christ then he or she already has.

How do we represent Christ to the postmodern? We approach them like we do any other unbeliever of any time, or culture, or language — we hand them the crucified and risen Savior. We bring them the essential.

APPENDIX

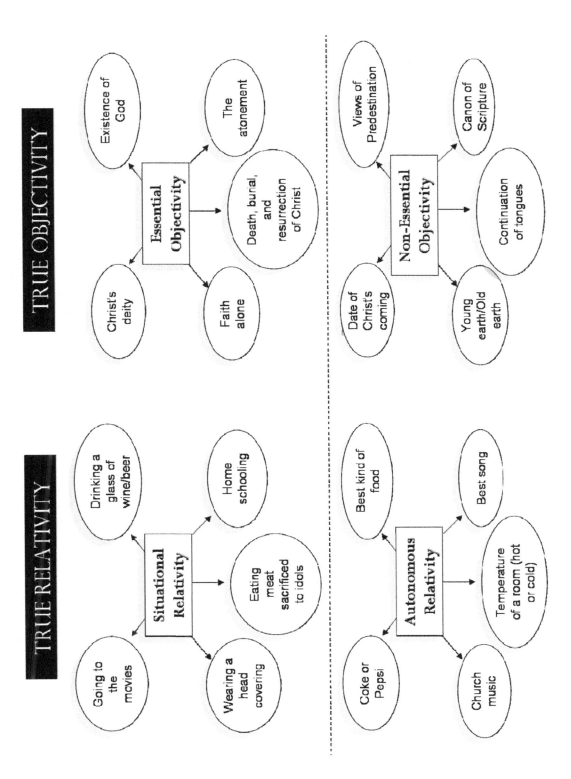

KEY TERMS FOR INTRODUCTION TO THEOLOGY (1)

1. **Irenic Theology**: Theology that is done peaceably, accurately representing all views, even when you oppose them.
2. **Polemic Theology**: Theology that is done in a warlike manner inside the Church, prophetically speaking against those with whom there is disagreement.
3. **Apologetic Theology**: Theology that is done to defend the faith against those who oppose outside the church.
4. **Prolegomena**: Literally means "things which are spoken beforehand." Deals with the foundational issues of theology, such as theological methodology, sources, and reasons for the study of theology.
5. **Bibliology**: The study of the nature, transmission, canonization, and purpose of Scripture.
6. **Theology Proper**: The study of God's nature, sometimes called "Trinitarianism."
7. **Christology**: The study of the person and work of Christ.
8. **Pneumatology**: The study of the nature and work of the Holy Spirit.
9. **Anthropology**: The study of the nature of humanity, both in its pre-fall and post-fall state.
10. **Soteriology**: The study of salvation.
11. **Ecclesiology**: The study of the nature of the Church.
12. **Hamartiology**: The study of sin.
13. **Eschatology**: The study of the last things.
14. **Evangelical**: A transdenominational term used to describe those within Christianity who believe that salvation is found in faith alone through Christ alone, and a commitment to Scripture as the inspired and infallible rule of life.
15. **Doctrine**: A theological formation that summarizes belief about a particular theological discipline.
16. **Dogma**: A statement of belief which carries with it the authority of a particular religious institution.
17. **Systematic Theology**: A system of studying theology which draws from all sources of revelation in order to come to systematic conclusions about what has been revealed about the various theological disciplines.
18. **Biblical Theology**: A system of studying theology that uses the Bible as its only source. Biblical theology can be done by looking at particular books, testaments, theology of a particular author, or the entire Bible as a whole.

KEY TERMS FOR INTRODUCTION TO THEOLOGY (2)

1. **Epistemology**: The study of the nature, existence, and acquisition of truth.
2. **Postmodernism**: A movement in modern society that devalues truth, believing all truth is relative.
3. **Universalism**: The belief that all will make it to Heaven.
4. **Pluralism**: The belief that there are many ways to God, most of which are equally valid.
5. **Syncretism**: The assimilation of differing beliefs and practices.
6. **Inclusivism**: The belief that salvation is only through Christ, but Christ may be revealed in other religions.
7. **Pragmatism**: The belief that truth is relative to its usefulness.
8. **Relativism**: The belief that truth is relative, dependent upon the situation or culture.
9. **Subjectivism**: The belief that truth is subjective, dependent upon the individual.
10. **Skepticism**: The belief that truth cannot be known with certainty.
11. **Objectivism**: The belief that truth is an objective reality that exist whether someone believes it or not.
12. **Perspectivism**: The belief that truth is found in the combined perspectives of many.
13. **Credo ut intelligum**: Lat. "Faith seeking understanding." This phrase was coined by St. Anselm and describes the Christian's endeavor to understand what he or she already believes. It is a good concise definition of what Christian theology truly is.
14. **Correspondence View of Truth**: The belief that truth corresponds to objective reality.
15. **Apophatic Theology**: Theology that emphasizes mystery.
16. **Cataphatic Theology**: Theology that emphasizes revelation.
17. **Special Revelation**: Revelation given by God's supernatural intervention in history through (1) miraculous events, (2) divine speech, and (3) visible manifestations.
18. **General Revelation**: Revelation that is natural and displayed by creation. It is available to all people of all times in all places.
19. **Hard Cessationism**: The view that the supernatural spiritual gifts ceased with the death of the Apostles.
20. **Continuationism**: The view that miraculous-sign gifts are still being given and, therefore, God still speaks directly in various ways today.
21. **Soft Cessationism**: The view that the miraculous-sign gifts could still be given today, but believers need to be careful about outright acceptance of people's claims of possession.
22. **semper reformanda**: The reformation principle that theology is "always reforming."

Made in the USA
Columbia, SC
13 September 2018